This fascinating and highly original study puts smell back on the psychoanalytic map, drawing together beautifully case study, autobiography, developmental theory, and conceptual analysis. Why has smell been neglected for so long despite being something that touches us all to the quick? Berjanet Jazani's arguments are compelling and the breadth of her examples are impressive, as we follow her reflections on the earliest role of smell in the bond of baby and mother to the place of breath in adult sexual practices. Every chapter of this superb book opens up new questions, enriching psychoanalytic theory and inviting us to lift the veil of repression that has blocked the exploration of this vital sensory pathway for so long.

— **Darian Leader**, *psychoanalyst, author*

At the risk of being outrageously cheeky, I will say that Berjanet Jazani has a nose for sniffing out what has been lost and radically under-theorised by psychoanalysis, until now. Selecting from ancient and interdisciplinary texts and theorists as well as from the Freudian and Lacanian oeuvres, scanding clinical vignettes from her own practice as well as dipping into her personal experiences, Jazani challenges contemporary psychoanalysis to speak of an olfactory drive in the same breath as the scopic and invocatory drives and to consider with her what is smell, what is breath, and what is the status of perfume and scent for the speaking being, in memory and mourning. With this work, we can say that Jazani restores the lost sense of smell to its rightful place, worthy, that is, of proper psychoanalytic scrutiny, and elevates olfaction convincingly for this reader to the status of the drive.

— **Carol Owens**, *psychoanalyst, Dublin*

Is there an olfactory drive, and if so, how does it work? By answering this question, Berjanet Jazani fills a huge gap in psychoanalysis' understanding of the undervalued sense of smell. Unlike other senses, olfactory perception requires a direct contact with the molecules that trigger chemical reactions in our brains. In a whiff, body and soul, brain and psyche, intermingle. This superb book full of arresting clinical examples puts us on the scent of an invisible mechanism that binds the aromas of the world to our unconscious.

— **Patricia Gherovici**, *psychoanalyst, author,*
Transgender Psychoanalysis

T0372803

The Perfume of Soul from Freud to Lacan

The Perfume of Soul from Freud to Lacan seeks to understand the human sense of smell and its marks on our subjectivity from a psychoanalytic perspective.

Accessibly written, the book considers whether our understanding of the sense of smell and odours in culture has changed over time, and where we locate olfaction in theories of psychoanalysis. Beginning with the theorisation of the sense of smell in philosophy and medicine, Berjanet Jazani explores what treatment of this sense we can find in historical and contemporary linguistic and cultural context. Jazani then takes examples from the psychoanalytic clinic as well as cultural references, from cinema to ancient literature, to elaborate the marks of the olfactory experiences on our subjectivity and sexuality. Lacanian theories, clinical anecdotes and autobiographical references are woven together to raise some critical questions about the law of odours as well as the invisible marks of breathing on subjective position, body, and symptom.

The Perfume of Soul from Freud to Lacan will be of great interest to psychoanalysts, academics, and all readers who are interested in psychoanalysis, philosophy, and culture.

Berjanet Jazani is a medical doctor and practicing psychoanalyst based in London, UK. She is the president of The College of Psychoanalysts UK, clinical member of the Centre for Freudian Analysis & Research (CFAR), and the author of *Lacanian Psychoanalysis from Clinic to Culture* and *Lacan, Mortality, Life and Language: Clinical and Cultural Explorations* (both Routledge).

The Perfume of Soul from Freud to Lacan

A Critical Reading of Smelling, Breathing and Subjectivity

Berjanet Jazani

Routledge
Taylor & Francis Group

LONDON AND NEW YORK

Designed cover image: Carlo Bollo/Alamy Stock Photo

First published 2025
by Routledge
4 Park Square, Milton Park, Abingdon, Oxon OX14 4RN

and by Routledge
605 Third Avenue, New York, NY 10158

Routledge is an imprint of the Taylor & Francis Group, an informa business

© 2025 Berjanet Jazani

British Library Cataloguing-in-Publication Data
A catalogue record for this book is available from the British Library

ISBN: 9781032779034 (hbk)
ISBN: 9781032757353 (pbk)
ISBN: 9781003485322 (ebk)

DOI: 10.4324/9781003485322

Typeset in Times New Roman
by KnowledgeWorks Global Ltd.

For Khosro, the scent of my homeland

Contents

Acknowledgements

This book arose from an everlasting scent, tied closely to the enduring image of a warm spring day in the midst of a mountain-desert region of Iran when I was 6 years old. At midday, driving through a desert, the cool shade of trees and bushes far away invited curiosity. Drawing nearer, we saw an oasis of vines and pear trees in full bloom. A gentle breeze from the shadow of the trees caressed my cheeks, and the silence of the scene held me captive. A swarm of white butterflies emerging from the trees made the beauty of the scene eloquent. The memory of their whiteness, appearing suddenly from the dark green background, leads to a memory of clusters of purple grapes that hung from the vines that were planted there and which I saw each year in the late summer before they were harvested for wine-making. But most powerful, intoxicating, evoking every desire for eternal joy and serenity was the scent of pear blossom. That scent stayed with me through long months when the coronavirus robbed me of the sense of smell. It gave life to the image of that place, which I call 'the Garden,' and led eventually, decades later, to the present book. Any number of odours come and go for us through life's journey, but there is usually one, which holds us and carries us away. Invoking the past, we step into a place that is most familiar to us: home. At the end, there is no scent to smell, and so there is no place to go and that is the end. To the scent of pear blossoms.

Also, to my dearest Khosro, without whom I could not have finished this book. In every breath we take, the smell of home is revived and relived. Counting the days to smell the air of our free Iran once again on an olfactory journey from the Austrian Alps to Iran's Zagros Mountains. Thank you, my Edelweiss!

To the sweet smell of sisterhood: to you always, Bernadette and Barsian.

To the smell of art which records moments: to you, Bardia.

To the remote yet close-to-home aroma of Lagerfeld Cologne: to memories of my father.

To the scent of womanhood.

To my grandmother who said that women are as soft as silk in their patience, as hard as jewels in their strong desire to nurture goodness and as fragrant as jasmine in their forgiveness of all the dire hardships that must face in life.

To the smell of mother and to my mother who loves delicate, powdery perfumes.

Last year, the smell of roses in my homeland was overpowered by the smell of grief and deep sadness. On 16 September 2022, a young Iranian woman, Mahsa (Jina) Amini, was brutally killed by the morality (Hijab) police of the Islamic regime while being held in custody. Mahsa's life was not the first or the last to be taken from Iranian women and men. Thousands of men, women, and children have been sacrificed to the stench of violent religious and ideological opportunism since 1979.

To the smell of freedom when we claim it back in the lands of a people that was free since ancient times – our Iran. The miasma of grief and mourning will be transformed into the breath of life, scented with joy.

To all women who have fought for their freedom and equal rights – not least for their free, scented hair. The freedom which was taken away from them in the last 44 years.

My sincere respect to the Shahbanou of Iran, H.M. Farah Pahlavi, and to every single mother, wife, partner, and sister of the men who were the victims of war and violence.

In an anxious letter addressed to Freud in the summer of 1932, Einstein had raised a couple of fundamental questions about the prevention of war in human society. He asks: 'Is there a way of freeing humankind from the threat of war? Can human aggression be channeled to help protect people against the impulses of hatred and destruction?'[1] (Einstein, 1932)

Freud in his response refers to the need for a recourse to violence to settle a conflict between two men. He goes on and gives a historical account of human evolution to point out the relation between human will, violence, and the need for ownership and authority. It is rather common knowledge that the envy between two parties is settled by seeking justice. The object of envy varies from one phallic value to another: power, money, other forms of possessions, and above all, ideologies and beliefs. Isn't it a usual way for siblings to seek justice through parental interventions in setting rules on rights? The parental intervention can vary from one cultural context to another, but the nature and essence of such a recourse to justice remain all the same. The outcome of how we respond to social rules and regulations depends on those interventions and our subjective interpretations of them. In other words, our ethical stance later in life originates from how we deal with our violent urges, as Freud reminds us.

1 https://en.unesco.org/courier/marzo-1993/why-war-letter-freud-einstein

For all the love and care they lavish and sacrifices they endure: to Tayebeh Ahrabian, Manijeh Rahimi, Sogol Ayrom, Dr Farrokhroo Parsa, Jaleh Kalantari, Nadereh Afshari, Azadeh Shafigh, Nayer Saeidi, Neda Aghasoltan, Mahsa Amini, Armita Geravand, Soheila Hejab, Vida Movahed, Nika Shakarami, Fatemeh Sepehri, Hadis Najafi, Sarina Esmaeilzade, and to the brave men, Navid Afkari, Pouya Bakhtiari, Majid Reza Rahnavard, and thousands more.

To the most beautiful fragrance: friendship. I would like to thank my friends Darian Leader, Mary Horlock, Loretta Monaco, Astrid Zecena, Viviane Blanchard, Andrew Hodgkiss, Carol Owens, Pat Blackett, Sepideh Pourkoushki, Ian Parker, Kalpa Roa, Pojhan Omidzohour, Abdi Rafatian, Annette Lyons, Vincent Dachy, Bice Benvenuto, Astrid Gessert, Mark Elmer, Anne Worthington, Simona Revelli, Alaleh Bahman, Andreea Goloca, Valentina Chiricallo and Mary Artemi, Anouchka Grose, and Shirin Alaghband.

A special thanks to my English editor, Ben Hooson, whose work and comments have always been insightful and helpful.

My sincere appreciation to those with whom I had meaningful conversation on the subject of olfaction and breathing: Natasa Bertalanic, Katy Gray, Anna Blazewska, Michelle Willett, Paul Gurney, Adina and Carla, Mehdi Baniasadi, Narges Sharifzadeh, Mohamad Fathi, Ehsan Goli, Mahdi Karimi, Maryam Mazaheri, and Susan Ghahremani.

A very special thanks to Susannah Frearson from Routledge. Her most kind and helpful advices and comments have always made my experience with this publishing house pleasant!

To the smell of Persian nights where noses are the host of a feast of floral fragrance until dawn.

And finally, to the myth of scents and songs, to the enduring love between the nightingale and the rose in Persian poetry (Gol o Bolbol).

Chapter 1

The Law of Odours

On Smells

In my childhood, there was a garden – I call it 'the Garden' – that had kept the aura of a lost paradise and the scent of Eden in the midst of a thirsty desert land. The Garden had come into being out of a drop of very precious perfume from the phial of time. The passage of time in that corner of heaven had found meaning through the earthy smell of cypress, almond, fig, vine, pear, quince, pomegranate and apricot trees, rooted in a salty land. The natural perfume of those trees was nourished by the soul of the soil, the kiss of the scorching sun and deep salty water. The distinctive sweet scent of pear blossoms in spring and fig leaves in summer gave way to the subtle sweet-sour fragrance of pomegranates and clusters of red and white grapes in autumn. Then, with the approach of winter, the air was rich with the aromas of pomegranate molasses and wine in the corner cellar of the Garden. This Garden of odours, in Kashan, Iran, was my safe space whenever we travelled there as visitors from the big city.

Smell is Time

I grew up with a hypersensitive nose. Odours, both sweet and foul, were my system of measurement. What found meaning for me through smell was not only time and space but also emotions, from love and joy to anger and anxiety, or the state of my own or other people's health (through the smell of breath or fever), the smell of mother (a warm, gentle touch of jasmine and lavender) and the smell of father (eau de cologne). Both of my parents were exceptionally sensitive towards smells and took pains to create and banish them. Their almost obsessional deodorising and re-odorising of body and environment surely determined my own sensitivity. In particular, my father's lavish use of perfume left me with a severe allergic reaction to any form of perfume until my early 20s, and my mother's obsession with de-odorisation played a role in my phobia of public toilets, which I avoided until adulthood, even at the cost of severe discomfort.

DOI: 10.4324/9781003485322-1

For me, the Garden was the only place where smells existed and could be enjoyed in freedom, without constraints and prohibitions.

Smell is Freedom

I distinctly remember the day when, more recently, I fell victim to COVID-19 and suddenly lost the ability to detect smells. At the time, I was working on my previous book, *Lacan, Mortality, Life and Language: Clinical and Cultural Explorations* (Jazani, 2021), finalising the manuscript before submission to the publisher. The balcony where I worked, facing a spectacular view of green mountains in the South of France, had a few pots of herbs. I reached for a pot of mint and breathed in. An electric sensation ran down to my spine as I realised that anosmia was among my symptoms. I reassured myself that it was only for a few days or weeks. It was actually much longer: 20 months without the power of olfaction (long COVID) was the most tasteless and senseless period of my life. Losing any sense is a great challenge, both physical and emotional, and I had lost the sense that is perhaps the most important to me for life and belonging. I checked for its return each day upon awakening until it gradually came back, but it never regained its former sharpness. My long anosmia was palliated by occasional olfactory dreams and hallucinatory reminiscences of the smell of food that my mother used to cook. The only clear gain from the experience was that a loss of pleasure (of the pleasure taken in olfaction) somehow helped me to work through grief over my father's death, which happened during the period of anosmia.

My own experience of losing the sense of smell is not the reason why I decided to study and write about olfaction. But it was a reminder of the paucity of psychoanalytic literature on the subject. Olfaction is not included in the list of the Freudian and Lacanian drives.

The Garden reappears in my writings as a lost paradise or lost *jouissance* – the fantasy of return does not fade. Its power lies in the multitude of associations which it has for me, what it represents to me and how it has marked my being. In my conscious memories and in my dreams, the home/homeland/ mother/love (the metonymic chain) has always been expressed/signified by a smell. In a recurrent dream after my self-imposed exile from Iran, I was searching for an exit from a looped circuit – the streets of a strange town. Finally, I breathed deeply and sensed the familiar smell of my home town, at which point I was able to wake up. My olfactory dreams were almost always related to my homeland.

A few years ago, I learned the history of the Garden. It had been a generational property until the premature and unfortunate death of my great grandfather. The Garden and other properties were sold and my grandfather, who was still a child, relocated elsewhere with his mother and siblings. When he had acquired some wealth, in his late 20s, he returned to his hometown and bought back the lands that had been sold, including the Garden. He took special care to recreate and care for Garden, and the trees that I have described above were tended long after his death as homage to his hard work and love for 'home'. I discovered this love through the smell of the Garden in its successive seasons. As Marcel Proust wrote:

> After people are dead, after the things are broken and scattered, taste and smell alone, more fragile but more enduring, more immaterial, more per-sistent, more faithful, remain poised a long time.
>
> (Proust, 1981, p. 47)

Smell is home and that, I think, is what gave me a fascination with olfactory experience and the desire to research and discuss it.

The project has proved challenging. My intention was to approach the olfactory sense from a psychoanalytic perspective. Half way through the work, I took a long break from it. My husband, Khosro, whose love for Iran is dedicated and enduring, gave me the strength to take it up again when he began a work of literature centred on the recent political history of our country. The smell of home was present again in our little corner of London and, back at my desk, I felt the Garden aromas of walnut, apple and mulberry as I finished my work on what I hope will be a prelude to future psychoanalytic works on olfaction and breathing.

Smell, the most primitive sense of all, is ever-present in our organic and speaking beings. It is the experience that is closest to home. In ancient literature, olfaction and odour figure more largely in philosophical texts than in works on medicine: the traces of Plato and Aristotle are ever-present in the medical works of Galen. For Galen, smell was one of the five external senses, placed in the midpoint of Galen's order of senses based on pleasure and pain: touch, taste, smell, hearing and sight. For Galen, the object of smell was situated between air and water, the idea being that odours arose when water changed to air and vice versa.

Plato listed four senses (he did not include touch) and ranked smell after taste. Aristotle went into more detail, listing different types of smell (sweet, sharp or hot, bitter, pungent and oily).

Avicenna focused on the quality of odours in terms of shape, size, movement, etc., and found that the olfactory sense is much less developed in human beings compared to other species. He also suggested that the object of perception is divided into two categories, material form and immaterial form, and placed smell in the latter group. While Galen distinguished the senses based on pleasure and displeasure, Avicenna's ranking is based on usefulness. Like Galen, he gave smell a ranking midway between the other senses. Thinkers from the 14th century onwards changed the order of the ranking but kept smell in the middle position. The Cartesian theorisation of the senses moved away radically from the ancient and medieval traditions, giving absolute primacy to vision.

Turning to religion, in Judaism and Christianity, smell and breathing were related to the division between heaven and hell, and, more fundamentally, the distinction between pleasant and unpleasant (the notion of God breathing spirit or essence into the human soul is recurrent). The common motif is that a sweet smell is both pleasant, healing and sacred. Zoroastrianism links religion to a medical and hygienic approach to smell, treating perfume as part of a purification process as well as a medical remedy.

In medieval texts, smell was a sign of power and social status as well as of sexuality and temptation. Foul smells were not only a sign of ill-health and death (as in times of plague) but also a stigma attached to strangers and foreigners: a token of xenophobia. The shape of the nose, the organ of olfaction, was also significant. Aristotle had claimed that people with long noses tended to be bold and brave, a hooked nose was a sign of courage and a nose like the beak of a crow indicated greed. A big nose was considered the sign of a judgmental character and a small nose suggested unreliability. According to Albertus Magnus, a pointed nose signified moral laxity, while a flat nose stood for voluptuousness. All of these suppositions took their cue from Aristotle. In past centuries, executioners slit the noses of those found guilty of sexual transgression, implying that the nose could be an organ of temptation. Much closer to our own times, the nasal reflex theory of Freud's one-time friend and collaborator, Wilhelm Fliess, claimed to find a direct link between nose and the genitalia. As can be seen, the nose was not only considered as a sensual organ but was also sexually metaphorised in language.

Discussing sensory education in *Émile or on Education,* Jean Jacques Rousseau wrote that the sense of smell ranks lowest among the senses due to the path followed by human evolution. Freud had a similar argument on olfaction when he made a connection between the anal drive and olfaction in modern man (there will be more to say about this). Rousseau had connected the sense of smell with imagination, believing that olfaction is stronger in women because they are more imaginative than men and claiming that children cannot be aroused by odours because their olfactory sense is not yet well developed. Rousseau treats olfaction exclusively in terms of evolution and sensuality, rather than as a sense that is transformed by man's nature as a speaking being (Rousseau, 1991).

What treatment of odours do we find in language? Olfaction as the most primitive sense is culture-bound: however, sophisticated the theorisation of the sense of smell in philosophy or cognitive science, the power of odours is experienced in a way that no knowledge can possibly teach. The power of involuntary, instant temporal and spatial transportation, provoked by a specific scent, traverses any conventional borders and boundaries. Meticulous and well-funded research by the perfumery industry has shown how certain scents can mend and transform people's mood.

Words can render a scent, so that the life of a scent as a sensual, bodily experience is extracted into language and then returned to the body, but perhaps with a different excitatory quality. Language kills the immediacy and primacy of the olfactory excitation, but that excitation finds a new life in language. Surely this is the logic at work when marketeers in the perfume business put as much effort into naming scents as their designers put into creating them. The choice of name for a perfume is intrinsic to fashioning an elixir that can supposedly restore youth, generate love and sexual attraction, cleanse the spirit or ward off demons, and it is not uncommon in our own shopping behaviour that we choose a perfume based on its name (not necessarily the brand name).

My first question in this book is – what exactly is smell? In medicine, theorisation of the sense of smell and odours dates back to Galen, whose ideas were greatly influenced by Plato and Aristotle, and who remained the most authoritative figure in western medicine through the Middle Ages and until 15th and 16th centuries. In Book VIII of *On The Function of the Parts*, Galen says that the olfactory organs are the anterior ventricles of the brain, where the nasal passages ascend. The olfactory passage is defined as: (1) olfactory areas in the nose; (2) pores in the ethnocide bone; (3) tubular nerves; (4) olfactory bulbs; (5) anterior (lateral) ventricles. The loss of smell was then attributed to blockage or disease in the olfactory passage or anterior ventricles.

In the Middle Ages, as anatomical knowledge gradually advanced, Bartholomeus Anglicus, a scholastic and the author of *On the Properties of Things* wrote that olfaction consists of: (1) olfactory nipples situated in the nose cavity and (2) the nerves that gather and carry impressions from the olfactory nipples to (3) the 'common sense' in the frontal ventricle of the brain. The medieval philosophical understanding of the human senses distinguished between the outer and inner senses. The outer senses were hearing, sight, taste, smell and touch. Input from the outer senses, received in the 'common sense' situated in the frontal ventricle, was believed to pass onwards through the inner senses, causing fantasy and imagination, before reaching the second ventricle, which was taken to be the centre of cognition and calculation. The final destination of sensual input was the third ventricle, where memories were created and stored. However, this depiction of the olfactory system still had more to do with Aristotelian natural philosophy than with medicine and anatomy (Palmer, 1993).

Further advances in human anatomy and the dissection of cadavers since the early 16th centuries produced more detailed knowledge of olfactory perception, particularly after the olfactory nerve was identified. The focus of medicine shifted to anatomy, clinical practice and individual case studies. A deeper understanding of the physiology of the sense of smell was only obtained quite recently. A French anatomist, Joseph–Hyppolite Cloquet, published a thesis in 1815 entitled *On Odours, the Sense of Olfaction and the Olfactory Organs*, and then wrote extensively on olfaction and diseases of the nose in his book *Osphresiology*, published in 1821, which is considered to be the first complete treaties on rhinology. Cloquet was the first to assert that odours are chemical molecules and to theorise the olfactory mucosa. However, Cloquet's work is not focused on scientific and physiological aspects of olfaction, and is most enlightening by virtue of its social and cultural references.

Through the 19th century researchers gave increasing attention to the study of the human chemosensory system and its role in the formation of odours. Human perception occurs when stimuli are transduced to action potential by receptors in the sensory organs. The action potential is transmitted to the cortex of the brain by afferent neurons. There are two types of receptors for such stimuli: exteroreceptors and interoceptors. Interoceptors receive stimuli from internal organs: all internal sensations, from breathing to gastrointestinal stimuli, blood flow, sugar level and many more are captured by interoceptors. Exteroreceptors are responsible for external sensations received by sense organs on the surface of the body and produce vision, hearing, touch and spatial orientation, taste, smell and balance. The sensory receptors are divided into photoreceptors, mechanoreceptors, thermoreceptors and chemoreceptors. The senses of smell and taste are both chemoreceptors. In physiology, the structure of the olfactory system consists of three parts: (1) the peripheral or olfactory sensory organ (the nose), where the olfactory epithelium receives odour molecules from the nostril or the back of the throat; (2) transduction, consisting of olfactory neurons that transmit information from the back of the nasal cavity to the brain; and (3) the central part of the olfactory system – the olfactory bulb and olfactory cortex. The olfactory part of the brain cortex includes the piriform cortex, amygdala, olfactory tubercle and parahippocampal gyrus. The role of the central part of the olfactory system is much discussed in the context of human cognitive behaviour (positive and negative reinforcement, sexual behaviour, rewarding and decision-making). Many neuroscientific studies have focused on trying to locate a connection between the central part of the olfactory system in the brain and human emotions and memories.

I am particularly interested in the relationship between language and olfaction. My research on the history of European and Iranian languages suggests that linguistic classification and qualitative descriptions of smells are based on a conventional correlation between each individual smell and an object. We may well wonder about the significance of this for our subjectivity from a psychoanalytic viewpoint. Smell also has a special place in the literature of various languages as a tool for describing, gauging and defining certain qualities, and for aesthetic purposes such as metaphorisng a sensation or an excitation. Smell, of all the senses, has a special correlation with intuition. Olfactory intuition in language, most notably in some ancient philosophical literatures, not only renders a meaning at the level of animalistic, instinctive or even cognitive awareness, but is literally equivalent to consciousness.

In this chapter, by unpacking different dimensions of smell as an olfactory experience as well as the object of olfaction, I aim, by following where a psychoanalytic nose leads, to investigate this sense as it marks our being. Different lines of thought about olfaction are followed in order to ascertain whether smell and smelling can be brought under the auspice of a certain analytic concept and, if so, what would be the consequence for clinical work with the subject of the unconscious.

'Can we smell art?' a friend wondered when we were discussing olfaction and psychoanalysis. She was referring specifically to the visual arts. She is an art historian and a fascination with history is the basis of her thought, politics and, as she puts it, her 'sense of being'. There must have been an unconscious desire at work that prompted me to share my project with someone who is so preoccupied with history. The sense of smell has great power for taking a subject on a journey into the past. No song, image or touch of a totem possess such power.

Our conversations expanded my knowledge on the work of some smell artists and perfumers, but the general question, which she posed, as to the smell of art perplexed us both. The question implied the possibility for someone to smell his or her way to enjoyment, as if to say that pleasure obtained through the scopic, tactile or invocatory drives is never enough.

The sense of smell no longer has the crucial role in the everyday life of human beings, which it had for our distant ancestors. In Chapter 3, I use examples from the clinic of psychoanalysis, works of literature and the medical understanding of olfaction to investigate the position or lack of position of the sense of smell in contemporary life. Olfaction has received much less attention in the analytic literature compared with the other senses. In this chapter, I highlight 'lost' or 'loss' in the sense, discussed above, of a lost paradise – a nostalgia, which is at the same time a necessary precondition for the subject to set off on their journey of life. In a Lacanian perspective, the object-cause-of-desire (*objet petit a*) is formulated as the remainder of an enjoyment, which has been cut off by language. This lost object is an excess or a forbidden *jouissance* located at the heart of the formation of the subject in language. Smell, as an ever-present sense, both forms and punctuates our mode of being. It is an essential element with an immortal and continuous character, affecting our lives.

Freud's major intervention regarding the sense of smell had to do with the anal drive and most psychoanalytic literature has paid more attention to foul than to pleasant odours, particularly in the clinic of perversion. This approach is contrary to that taken by other literature. Generally, bad smells have received different treatments in different cultures. In some cultures, it is considered socially unacceptable to even mention foul odours. In most languages, specific smells, unlike colours, can only be defined indirectly, by reference to the objects that produce them. One exception is the language of Jahai- and Thai-speaking hunter gatherers in northern Malaysia, who have dedicated abstract terms for odours. For Françoise Dolto, the mother's body was recognised by the infant through two main senses: smell and voice, where smell signals the mother's proximity and her voice signals her distance. Dolto reminds us that the smell of mother's body is reassuring to the infant. But what does such reassurance mean and what are we to make of the mother's skin as drive object? Would it not be more logical to associate reassurance with being safely held, hence with the tactile drive rather than the smell of the skin?

The sense of smell is a *sine qua non* of our awareness of our own sexualised and mortal body, and of our identification, alienation and separation from the Other. It also has a substantial role in our social bond with other people. Olfaction not only has a pronounced presence in our physical being: we learn from the clinic of psychoanalysis how this instinctual, intuitive and primitive sense has formative effects on our mode of being in language as subjects of the unconscious. Such major presence of olfaction in both consciousness and the unconscious makes the lack of psychoanalytic discussion of the sense of smell very striking. Moreover, it is hard to find a way of approaching and locating this primitive sense in existing psychoanalytic theories. The most obvious place for olfaction in psychoanalytic theories would be the concept of drive. We should then wonder why psychoanalysts have not spoken of an olfactory drive in the same breath with which they have spoken of the scopic and invocatory drives (related to sight and hearing). As I said earlier, this is, in fact, the central question to be pursued in the present research. Freud (himself a life-long and heavy smoker) worked with patients who complained of olfactory hallucinations (the smell of burnt pudding in Lucy R's case), *renifleurs* (the Ratman) and cases of coprophilia. So why did he not treat this sense as worthy of classification among the drives? It was Lacan who added the scopic and invocatory drives to Freud's list of the drives, while at the same time remaining faithful to Freud's approach to the concept of the drive as such drive and its 'vicissitudes'. We know that Lacan's intellectual journey in psychoanalysis starts from sight (his theorisation of the mirror stage in the 1930s). The specular image gives meaning to the first of the three Lacanian registers: the Imaginary. And yet it is common knowledge that odours (the object of smell) are the most powerful of the stimuli that make us retrieve screen memories, imagine things and be catapulted into the past. Or, as one of my students once said, 'the past is catapulted to us'. Is it the acquisition of language that has led the subject of the unconscious to renounce reliance on his instincts?

In Chapter 4, I try to see if olfaction can in fact be brought under the auspices of the concept of the drive. Could we consider olfaction as a separate montage of the drive in the concept of human sexuality? How can such a formulation help our understanding of olfaction from a psychoanalytic viewpoint? And, again, how would such a stance affect our clinical work? I use clinical anecdotes involving olfaction in order to elaborate on these questions. As might have been expected, the clinic of the human subject tends to complicate any simplistic approach to the subjective phenomena encountered on the couch.

In Chapter 5, I ask, 'what is breathing?' and try to explore a neglected dimension of the act of inhaling and exhaling air. To do so may seem to depart from the focus of the book, as breathing can stand alone, independent of olfaction, but olfaction without respiration is, of course, impossible and the very fact that smelling happens through breathing in a speaking being should provoke thought. If the olfactory faculty was located in another part of our body, perhaps the effect of olfaction on our subjectivity would have altered accordingly. But this last chapter also considers respiration as a vital autonomous process, not solely in the light of olfaction, and a new book project could perhaps be dedicated to the subject of breathing. I try to highlight certain qualities of breathing in order to better understand how the foundational concept of being alive depends for a subject on the air that he or she breathes in and out, elaborating the impact of a narrative around the act of breathing (and breathing as itself a narrative) on the formation of the subject of the unconscious.

Inhaling and exhaling air, whether fragrant (giving pleasure to the subject) or foul and miasmic (perhaps with ill-effect on health), generates a boundary of our being – inside and outside. It is an act that happens continuously and unconsciously. Olfaction and taste, unlike other sensory faculties (tactile, scopic and auditory) are on both sides of the border that separates our body from what is outside it. The other three senses can only signify the outer border of our body, distinguishing our corporeal mass from what surrounds it. Breathing and smell proceed without conscious awareness and their autonomy is a challenge to the authority of the subject over olfaction. We breathe in and experience smells whether we want to or not, unless we intervene consciously and either hold our breath or breathe only through our mouth, which is unsustainable for long periods of time.

The chapter on respiration closes this book which will, I hope, continue to respire and offer a starting point for other psychoanalysts and those who are interested in psychosocial and cultural studies to be intrigued by the subject of olfaction and breath. In the new environment where artificial intelligence and robotics are part and parcel of our cultural habitat, we may see the emergence of an 'AI nose' and olfactory culture may see much alteration. Breathing could find a new resonance at organic and linguistic levels, impacting our mode of being. How can psychoanalysis respond to the new cultural changes? Sentient robots will surely make the concepts of belonging and home, which are so closely related to olfaction, into something different, generating marks on a new form of subjectivity.

No sense is ever just a sense. Once the word meets our organic body, the body is no longer merely organic. It is altered forever. The sense of smell stands out among all the senses due to its intrinsic bond with breathing – the mark of life, – a bond that entails going beyond borders and agency. Above all, the sense of smell is the sense of belonging.

To the scents of life.

Berjanet Jazani

September 2023, Vienna, Austria

Bibliography

Jazani, B. (2021). *Lacan, Mortality, Life and Language: Clinical and Cultural Explorations*. London: Routledge
Palmer, R. (1993). In Bad Odour: Smell and Its Significance in Medicine From Antiquity to the Seventeenth Century. pp. 61–69. In: *Medicine and the Five Senses*, Bynum, W. F. & Porter, R. (eds). Cambridge: Cambridge University Press
Proust, M. (1981). *In Search of the Lost Time: Vol.1 Swann's Way*. London: Everyman Publishers plc
Rousseau, J. J. (1991). *Emile; or on Education*. London: Penguin

Chapter 2

What is Smell?

Introduction

The mere absence of an offensive smell from the body and breath was as pleasing to Montaigne as a sweet fragrance: 'The best we can hope for is to smell of nothing,' he says. He acknowledged his enjoyment of living among good smells, but nothing pleased him better than the mild and natural smell of a healthy body. He suspected that people who cover their body with expensive perfumes stink the most. Clearly, he was a sceptical philosopher as regards perfumes. He theorised smell as a marker of health and the treatment of illness, of religious purification (the use of scents in churches), gender difference (the distinction between the genders in Montaigne's time was based largely on bodily odours), as having a close affinity with the sense of taste (the oral drive) and finally, since malodourous air was considered to be the cause of illness, he was of the opinion that choice of place to live should depend on the smell of the air. So, for Montaigne, our sense of space was associated with olfaction. Socrates was like Montaigne in disdaining the use of perfumes. However, in ancient society there was another logic at stake, since perfumes could disguise the olfactory differences between free citizens and slaves (Classon, 1994).

Jean Jacques Rousseau wrote in *Émile* that smell has the lowest rank of all the senses, justifying his idea with references to human evolution in a way that perhaps predicts what Freud had to say about olfaction and the anal drive-in modern man. Rousseau also links the sense of smell to the imagination. So, for him, olfaction is stronger in women because they are more imaginative. He believed that children cannot be excited by odours because their other senses are not yet sufficiently well developed. Rousseau deals with olfaction in terms of evolution and sensuality rather than as a sense, which has been transformed for a speaking being (Rousseau, 1991).

It is believed that the principal role of smell in pre-history was for detecting food, identifying threats and mating behaviour, or, in a word, to keep the human race from extinction. The development of language in human societies has complicated sensory experience for the subject of the unconscious, which

DOI: 10.4324/9781003485322-2

came into being with the advent of language. The Freudian theory of the drive was the first attempt to theorise the subjective function of the sensory field in speaking beings. We will discuss and elaborate the concept of the drive in more detail in the chapter devoted to the olfactory drive.

Human beings have always tended to preserve, retain and go back to whatever generates enjoyment for them. Many innovative ideas and inventions in the history of science can be seen as responses to such an original urge. Technologies that record images and sound effects are obvious examples. More recently, information technologies have enabled us to recreate the voices, noises and look of the Ancient World. Olfaction, however, is the most naturally preserved form of the senses and can extend backwards as far as recorded history and beyond. We do not need technological recreation of the smell of the Ancient World to tell us how wood, sea, roses, rotten carcasses, etc. smelt thousands of years ago. The objects of olfaction, odour and scents that we have here and now let us be time travellers without needing a time machine!

Smell is the most powerful and intuitive among all types of sensory experience in a dialectical relationship between the subject and the Other, from the smell of the first significant Other, the mOther, to the smell of food and excrement, carrying a form of narrative while punctuating the subject's relationship with the mOther, temporal and spatial metrics and, most importantly, their own body as the first Other. Smell is the most powerful marker of the past as well as leaving a mark at the level of the formation of the subject. Smell has a leading role in our relationship with the past and with historical life events. An olfactory stimulus can catapult us into the past, even when we are not actively searching for a particular memory. Although it is often considered as what is most evanescent in the presence of the care giver and in the subject's own presence (as compared with visual image, milk, voice and skin), smell is in fact the most profoundly preserved sense as a marker of being in the field of the subject and the Other. Such a complex power should make us ask *what is smell?* What is the status of olfaction for a speaking being whose existence and mortality finds a new meaning at the level of culture, influenced by language?

At another level of presence, in the dream work, smells and tastes are frequent references alongside images, sound and touch, in a subject's account of their dreams. Let us start with a clinical anecdote to show the complexity of the meaning and function of olfactory experience from a psychoanalytic viewpoint.

Freud believed that the process of mourning can be manifested in a subject's dreams and it is not uncommon in the clinic of psychoanalysis to hear of olfactory experiences in the patient's dreams after they have lost someone close to them. A patient of mine who started analysis soon after losing her father reported that she was not able to see her father in her current dreams, but she sensed her father's familiar smell before or upon waking up. So, she was reassured of her father's presence in the dream through an olfactory experience, even though there was no image of him in any of the dream scenes. As her grief was processed over time, she recounted to me in a session that she had begun to see her father in her dreams and she no longer made mention of his familiar smell. It was as if the replacement in her dreams of olfactory sensation by sight marked the passing of the acute stage of her grief. The suggestion is that smell is a primitive sensual experience, more powerful than sight. It emerged from exploration of her earlier life events that she had been an anxious and temperamental child and had a very difficult relationship with her mother. She was often angry and dissatisfied with her mother, and had experienced some paranoid phases in respect of her since childhood. She also remembered finding it difficult to focus on her studies and being hyperactive at school. Her parents had separated soon after her birth and she saw her father at weekends or during school holidays. A significant memory of her relationship with her father was of falling asleep quickly and peacefully in his arms. Olfaction had a significant presence in the accounts she gave of her childhood experiences. She had felt a calmness and used to fall asleep easily when she sensed her father's smell. Much later in life, after her father died, she told me that the only memento she selected from her father's belonging was his shirt, which carried his smell. From a Lacanian perspective, we might say that her father's smell was a marker of his name (the Name of the Father). It was a marker with a magical power, carrying an inscription from the past that had a reassuring interpretation for the subject.

Another case extract with an olfactory reference shows again why there is more to olfaction than a mere sensory, corporeal perception and that olfaction cannot be pinned down to a conventional functionality. In a case of anorexia, a subject had developed the habit of satisfying her hunger by the smell and flavour of certain foods. She went shopping for food flavours instead of actual food. The avoidance of eating, after a painful breakup with her boyfriend, was her way of coping with separation – a theme that went back much further in her life history. Seen from the outside, she had replaced food by the object of olfaction (smell) as the oral object. But why smell could function for her in this way remained an open question and the particular type of smell (food flavour) that she chose offered a starting point for the analyst to tackle the question of enjoyment in a meticulous manner. The food flavourings she chose were mainly 'basic flavours' (banana, apple, cinnamon, vanilla and butter), which can be found in most baby foods. She added them to water or other low-calorie liquids, which she consumed. Further investigation revealed elaborate toiletry and defecation rituals, which she had developed since her teenage years. She had almost zero tolerance for unpleasant bodily smells, either her own or other people. These avoiding habits might suggest that she would live more happily and easily without her sense of smell. And yet her libidinal investment of this sense (her displaced eating habit, and also extravagant use of perfumes) indicated strong dependence on it. What was smell for her? Was it a proxy or a shield punctuating her distance from the Other, giving meaning to her existence, or was it simply an enjoyment derived from her olfactory faculty?

In this chapter, I want to try to unpack different dimensions of smell as an olfactory experience and think about the nature of the object of olfaction. How has this sense been theorised in medicine and philosophy and how can a 'psychoanalytic nose' investigate this sense as a phenomenon that marks our being? How can psychoanalysis respond to the question of what smell is? I will consider various lines of thought about olfaction and raise questions on the available formulations of the olfactory experience. Can smell and smelling be firmly placed under the auspice of a particular analytic concept? How could such a formulation affect the clinic of the subject of the unconscious?

Smell in the History of Medicine

Science, including the science of medicine, has a quite straightforward answer to the question, 'What is smell?' Olfaction is defined as a chemo-receptor. When odour molecules bind with specific sites in the nasal cavity, signals are sent to the olfactory bulb, where the olfactory input interacts with a specific part of the brain. Olfactory dysfunction can be central (arising in the brain or nervous system) or peripheral (arising in the sense organs). Examples of the first type include traumatic brain injuries, neurodegenerative illnesses, such as Parkinson's and Alzheimer's disease, and congenital conditions. There are numerous clinical reports of loss of the sense of smell in severe cases of anorexia and depression, and the direction of causality is often in question in such cases (anxious or/and depressive moods may be the result and not the cause of the loss). We will come back to the question of loss of olfaction later in this and the next chapter.

Humans, like other mammals, have the ability to perceive and code odours with relatively few active genes responsible for processing a wide range of odours. Researchers have recently developed a number of theories that attempt to define how olfaction works. They focus mainly on the features, volume and vibrating frequency of odorants when combining with smell receptors. The olfactory system in humans, as in other vertebrates, is tied into the respiratory system. So, the sense of smell is dependent on breathing. I will examine in a later chapter how and to what extent the olfaction-respiration linkage can affect how we perceive our subjectivity as a speaking being.

Since antiquity, the sense of smell has been considered important for proper evaluation of the aetiology, epistemology, prognosis and diagnosis of an ailment. Also, any condition that inhibits or disables the sense of smell has been regarded as a serious illness. The author of *Affections* (one of the works of the Hippocratic Corpus) blames the smell of bad air as one of the possible causes of an imbalance in the bodily humours (mainly phlegm and bile), which results in illness. 'Miasmata', which include pollution from a noxious haze arising from the decomposition of organic matter, was believed to cause physical and psychological illnesses. An ill-smelling substance or malodorous air was even supposed to be the direct cause of death. There was an idea that humans were particularly vulnerable to contamination by the smell of bad air, due to their more vital dependence on respiration compared to eating, drinking, and sexual and non-sexual touch. The influence of the harmful object could pass inside the subject's body through smell (via inhalation) as easily or more easily than through noxious foods and drinks, and much more immediately than by touch. What we take into our body through orality can be controlled more than what we take in through respiration. The invisibility of smell was another factor that made it into a mysterious and powerful phenomenon.

Philosophers, from the ancient Greeks onwards, have also had much to say about the sense of smell. In ancient Greece, the organ of olfaction was generally taken to be the nose (not the brain), However, Hippocrates and Galen dissented from this belief and asserted that the sense of smell depends on the brain. Later, anatomical and neurological findings supported their theories.

In Galenic medical texts, the terms used to describe different types of odours indicating health or ailment were limited to the Aristotelian dichotomy of pleasant and unpleasant smells. Similar to emotions and feelings in the Platonic classification, the language used to deal with olfaction tends to be comparative and descriptive. For example, the bodily smells, which were considered important for correct medical diagnosis were described in terms of culinary odours (garlic, fish, rotten food, etc.).

The use of perfumes as remedies (belief in the pharmaceutical qualities of odours) was important to the ancients. Aromatic fires were used to cleanse bad air at least from the time of Hippocrates. Theriac or Venice treacle (a concoction of aromatics and fermented herbs) was used in the Ancient World as a means of preventing and curing the plague. The medicinal use of perfumery continued through the Middle Ages. For instance, during the great plague of 1348, the use of cold and hot aromatics (in summer and winter, respectively) was recommended as protections against infection, the idea being to keep a balance between body and air. Related to the fear of breathing bad air, any intervention, which could potentially open the pores of the skin was highly discouraged as it was believed that infection could enter the body through such pores. Heat and humidity were considered dangerous because inhaled air was more likely to be polluted under such circumstances. The faculty of medicine in Paris recommended the sprinkling of aromatics such as rosewater or vinegar in summer in order to keep illness away. In Persian medicine, rose water was used to cool and temper humidity in the body. In winter time various aromatics with a 'warm' quality, such as musk, ambergris or sweet gum were used to balance room temperature and humidity (Le Guerer, 1992).

The clinic of psychoanalysis places the emphasis on matters of olfaction differently from mainstream medicine. The psychoanalyst is not so focused on the qualitative or quantitative consequences, which a subject face when they lose their ability to smell, or, on the contrary, when they experience hypersensitivity to olfactory stimuli or olfactory hallucinations. In such cases, it is, in fact, in the absence of ordinary olfactory sensation that the smell finds a significance for the analytic interpretation. The analytic ear listens to the analysand's narratives around such changes in their olfactory experience in order to detect a subjective interpretation formed much earlier in life. Such an interpretation has a constitutive role in the formation of the symptom, which gives meaning to the subject's being. How a subject reacts to such olfactory dysfunction and the narratives, which are produced in such circumstances are the questions that interest psychoanalysis. From a psychoanalytic perspective, olfactory dysfunctionality points at the Real aspect of the body and this is the target of an analytic interpretation. The concept of the Real body is elaborated in my previous book, *Lacan, Mortality, Life and Language: Clinical and Cultural Explorations* (Jazani, 2021). In anosmia (loss of the sense of smell) or in olfactory hallucination, the subject endures a loss – either loss of the ability to sense smells, or loss of the literal object of smell, which has failed to be symbolised and comes back to the subject from the Real in the form of hallucination. How such a loss affects the subject of the unconscious is the principal and the first question to be asked. Through this question, smell finds a meaning in the subject's narrative. Here, the analytic approach does not intersect with the medical understanding of the question, 'What is smell?' Smell in the clinic of psychoanalysis is also a bodily event, but not an event of the 'medicalised' body. One of Freud's early clinical cases that of Lucy R. in the *Studies on Hysteria* of the mid-1890s, presents olfactory symptoms. The patient suffered from chronic suppurative rhinitis, which was followed by loss of sense of smell, but she complained of subjective olfactory sensations and particularly the smell of burnt pudding. A colleague referred the patient to Freud after being unable to find evidence of a medical condition. Freud linked Lucy's subjective sensations to her depression as an affect resulting from a traumatic event, assuming that there might have been an objective experience that incidentally involved smell and that the recurrent olfactory hallucination was a way of symbolising what was traumatic in the memory of that experience. He treated the olfactory hallucination as a hysterical attack and the case as one of conversion hysteria. After Freud's interventions, Lucy acknowledged to Freud that she was in love with the father of the children, whom she was taking care of as a governess. Freud concluded that Lucy had repressed psychical excitation from her conscious associations and the repressed material had returned as a somatic manifestation (distantly connected with her unrequited love and the associated disappointment) in a way that was typical of conversion hysteria. He writes:

> … an idea must be intentionally repressed from consciousness and excluded from associative modification. In my view, this intentional repression is also the basis for the conversion, whether total or partial, of the

sum of excitation. The sum of excitation, being cut off from psychical association, finds its way all the more easily along the wrong path to a somatic innervation.

(Freud, 1893, p. 116)

Later, the smell of burnt pudding was replaced by the smell of cigar smoke, which could also be connected with a scene related to her unrequited love. Freud concluded that her subjective olfactory sensation/hallucination (smell of burnt pudding) was, in fact, a symptom that had been replaced by another symptom (smell of cigar smoke). To Freud, her olfactory hallucination was a replaceable symptom resulting from a repressed excitation in the psyche. Such a symptom defends the subject against an unbearable trauma.

This clinical picture where a somatic olfactory experience has such major presence leads us to ask why Lucy had developed subjective excitations (a hallucinated smell of burnt pudding/cigar smoke) further to her loss of sense of smell? Why did she suffer from persistent rhinitis, and why was there a libidinal investment in the nose and in breathing? Why the hallucinated smell was the smell of a particular object (burnt pudding)? Did it have a significance at the level of her earlier life narratives? From a reference to a letter received from her mother in the case study, Lucy seems to have had an affectionate relationship with her mother. On the other hand, she loved the children of her employer. Was the key factor her love towards the man, which Freud highlighted, or was it the feminine enjoyment of being a mother? As can be seen, in a clinical case that is viewed from a psychoanalytic perspective a smell (in this case, hallucinated) offers more complications than a marker of health or illness. But even if we agree on the status of the smell as a Freudian symptom, what does that symptom (olfactory sensation) mean for a subject? What is really communicated through the olfaction? I will consider another famous case study with olfactory references from Freud's work – the case of the so-called 'Rat Man' – further on.

Smell in Cultural Context

Philosophical thinking treats smell as a socio-cultural phenomenon. Any talk about olfaction is the product of a culture and an olfactory narrative forms a discourse, usually in everyday (non-specialised) language. Constance Classen, in her book, *Aroma: The Cultural History of Smell*, explores the meaning, function and power of smell since the Ancient World. She notes that scent has always been a discriminatory indication of gender and social status, as well as functioning as a border between cities and spaces. The use of perfume by men and women was part of their interpretation of the difference between day and night. Odour has been used down the ages in literature to express subtleties of scene and personality, making particular pleasant or unpleasant smells into

markers of conditions, career or even age. For instance, old age and prosti-
tution have been described as 'malodorous'. Most ancient philosophers (all
male) judged that women's odour was foul, perhaps extending a common
belief about witches. Since foul smell was a phobic object for centuries of
human history, believed to have the power to pollute air and water, causing
plague and destruction, we may suspect an association with men's fear of the
power of women to conceive and reproduce (Classon, 1994).

A person's having or not having control over their olfactory perception
can play a role at the level of the meaning, importance and impact, which
the olfactory sense has for a subject. Smelling comes with breathing. We will
explore and elaborate the idea of breathing as a *sine qua non* of olfaction in
more detail in the next chapter. But it is obvious at once that without breathing
we lose olfactory perception. Breathing is a reflex, which our brain controls.
What we automatically breathe in comes or does not come with a smell. Most
of the air pollutants and harmful particles in the modern world do not have
any smell. As we have seen, in the Ancient World, bad air or 'miasma' was
blamed for many diseases and for outbreaks of cholera or plague. Miasma
theory treated malodorous air as if the odour was itself what we today would
call a dangerous germ ('malaria' in medieval Italian means 'bad air'). The
fact that the subject has to breathe and therefore cannot help inhaling a bad,
disease-causing smell made olfaction into a mysteriously powerful sense, a
sense with the power of life and death. We can avoid a disturbing or harmful
sound by walking away or closing our ears, and we can just as easily choose
not to touch, see or taste something that we believe to be harmful, but the
need to breathe makes a smell much harder to escape. So, affliction by an
airborne disease appeared to be a matter of fate or destiny and death from
breathing poisonous air was more feared than death from swallowing poi-
son, because there was much less chance of active avoidance in the former
case. The subject's agency in seeing, hearing, touching and swallowing is
greater than in breathing, by which smell infiltrates the body without having
to cross a boundary. At the level of the mother-child relationship, smell comes
with breathing before the new-born relates to the external world by any other
means. It is true that during and soon after labour, the new-born is touched and
held. However, while tactility and being held come initially from the mOther's side, breathing is the first active contact made by the child (subject) when
they enter the world. The question whether a smell is pleasant or unpleasant
surely does not arise for a newborn infant, but the olfactory experience, which
comes with breathing in the air can have an interpretation for the subject to
be. The fragrance of the mOther's skin, of her breath, of the baby's own body
and its excrement, the smell of milk (mother's or bottled) can all be perceived
as experiences with meanings beyond mere corporeal stimulus. The feeling
of the mOther's presence, the promise of being fed or held, being reassured
of warmth (physically and emotionally) can originate for the child from the
smell of the mOther. So, smell is the most primitive sense and olfaction has

a principal role in forming our mode of being as a speaking and social being. This formulation will be our focus in Chapter 3 where the sense of smell is approached through a rhetorical question: 'Smell: a lost sense?'

One aspect of the power of odours, since ancient times, has concerned the question of mortality and divinity. The sweet smell of gods and goddess, and then, in European Christianity, the smell of sanctity and divine presence, has functioned as a sanctioning element for the power of the king, queen or head of state. The ritual use of scented oils by the newly appointed monarch shows the political aspect of smell. Burning the bodies of criminals and witches to make the stench of sin disappear is another example of the powerful socio-political importance of smell. On the other hand, the prohibition of the use of incense and fragrance at various times in the history of religion shows how the status of odour in human society had been transformed from something with a mainly instinctual nature to a cause of pleasure. The temptation to enjoyment was felt to be at odds with religious doctrine. Generally, we see a range in the use of perfume and fragrances from personal indulgence to attachment to higher beings (saints, God or heaven itself), the latter following on from times before monotheism, when pleasant or appetising smells were sometimes generated as offerings to the gods.

As will be discussed later in this book, the role of perfumes has transformed through history from medical uses to uses associated with socio-cultural status. In the past, perfume was a way of protecting people from inhalation of infectious air, particularly during the time of the plague in Europe ('perfume' literally means 'through smoke'). In England in the Middle Ages, people were advised to carry pomanders or perfume balls to protect themselves from bad air, which was believed to be the cause of plague. Specifically, the stench of putrefaction was believed to be the main cause of contamination. The pomander was a mixture of ambergris, musk and civet carried in a special container, like a piece of jewellery or a small bag. Smothering the bad smell or saturating the body's respiratory system with a perfume were the supposed solutions for preventing contamination.

The idea of contamination is itself thought provoking. As discussed earlier in the present chapter, olfaction and, to a lesser degree, tactility were historically the focus of preventive medicine. We may well wonder about the contradictoriness of smell in this regard. One smell was treated as an antidote to another smell that was a source of illness and misery. The one was therapeutic, while the other was destructive. The same paradox applied to some extent for tactility, when patients were advised to smear their bodies with certain ointments or remedies or even the skin's own dirt in order to obstruct contamination by an illness, which was supposed capable of penetrating the pores of the skin in order to enter the body, so that a wholesome tactile experience countered one that was baleful. Avoiding the so-called 'demons' that caused illness or threatened a subject's health was supposed to be far easier for oral and sexual contaminations due to the degree of control that a subject can exercise over access to his or her body via sex or ingestion. Not eating/ tasting or avoiding sexual or tactile contamination is easier than preventing olfactory contamination where the agent of death is in the air we breathe. Even holding one's breath as an intentional act cannot save the subject from contamination by the toxic airborne particles. So, the question how much agency can be exercised over olfaction compared with other senses is a key factor in understanding its nature and status.

In the study of mental illness as opposed to physical illness, sight and hearing have been given more attention than olfaction. This is also true of socio-political, cultural and philosophical takes on mental well-being. Very broadly, watching, listening and, to a lesser extent, smelling what is considered aesthetically pleasant have been considered both preventive and curative of mental illnesses.

All of the sensual faculties receive equal treatment when it comes to practices of abstinence in certain religious doctrines. Any temptation to pleasure originating from the visual, vocal, olfactory and tactile senses and from taste is condemned with the exception of particular circumstances, which are sanctioned by a superior holy presence (the Other). In Shia Islam, women are only allowed to wear perfume in the presence of their husbands and a pleasant artificial fragrance emanating from a woman is considered to be sinful. So, the metonymic chain here goes from smell as fragrance to woman, temptation and sin. In such an approach to the question 'What is smell?' olfaction is interpreted as sensuality. One might speculate here on a similarity between the angle from which psychoanalysis approaches the different faculties of sense, and the approach taken by some religions. I will elaborate the specifics of the analytic take on olfaction in the chapter, 'Is there an olfactory drive?'

From an analytic perspective, pleasure and enjoyment are far from being the same thing. Psychoanalysis does not believe in a well-defined and structured pleasure principle, as testified by Freud's challenging paper, *Beyond the Pleasure Principle* (Freud, 1920). What is the implication of this for olfaction in our social being today? We live at a time when the use of perfume is no longer medicinal, and the emphasis is on the aesthetic side of pleasant fragrances and perfumes, entailing a different definition of olfactory enjoyment. Firstly, branding and advertising strategies in the perfume market attempt to reduce the meaning of enjoyment to the pleasure principle. Baudrillard's concept of hyperreality can perhaps offer a way of understanding how the essential meaning and function of smell in our everyday life have been altered and emptied out in a market-based society. Although new marketing strategies, unlike those of the 20th century, promote 'natural' and 'subtle' fragrances, the extent to which this approach really wants us to stop fearing or even to appreciate the natural odours in our environment is doubtful to say the least. Fragrances that are labelled under such headings as 'freshness' or 'cleanness', usually have very little to do with real smells of the natural world. Our preferences in matters of fashion, including fragrance fashion, is inevitably dependent on advertising and, to an even greater extent, on politics. Is it really our own choice to have or not have certain fragrances (perfumes, candles, air fresheners, fragrant soaps, etc.) on our shopping list? How far is our olfactory pleasure engineered to accord with the dictates of the market? The name and image associated with a particular odour give a meaning to it. The descriptive name fabricated and offered by a particular brand defines the olfactory experience.

Psychoanalytic Understanding of Smell

Does the contribution of psychoanalytic literature to the understanding of the sense of smell only concern a pleasure found in the expression of the sexual drive, or are there psychoanalytical references to this sense that are less directly linked to sexual satisfaction? In the rest of this chapter, we will focus on Freud's work in the late 19th century and early 20th centuries, particularly his 'Ratman' case history, in order to raise some questions about the widely accepted interpretation of the meaning and role of smell in the clinic of psychoanalysis, an interpretation, which remains important in the work of post-Freudians to this day. In Chapter 3, we will go further into the psychoanalytic significance of olfaction by examining how this sense is ever present in the everyday life of our civilization, not only as a source of enjoyment and not only a formative element of our sexuality, but as a marker of our presence/absence as a sexed and social being. Smell is a silent but full narrative of the Real body that leaves a mark at the level of the subject's formation and relationship with the Other.

Freud asked whether the change of human posture to an upright position, by reducing the instinctual pleasure to be had from olfaction, might explain why human sexual life fell victim to repression and might thus play a role in the phylogenesis of neurosis. He writes:

> … And here I should like to raise the general question whether the atrophy of the sense of smell (which is an inevitable result of man's assumption of an erect posture) and the consequent organic repression of his pleasure in smell may not have had a considerable share in the origin of his susceptibility to nervous disease. This would afford us some explanations of why, with the advance of civilization, it is precisely sexual life that must fall a victim to repression. For we have long known the intimate connection in the animal organisation between the sexual instinct and the function of the olfactory organ.
>
> (Freud, 1909, p. 248)

The Ratman – the subject of Freud's famous case history of an adult obsessional neurosis – was a 'renifleur'. As a young child, he used to recognise people by the smell of their clothes. In his original record of the Ratman case (discovered and published long after publication of the case history), Freud notes on December 12th 1907 that the Ratman had told him that he also took pleasure in the smell of women's hair and on that same date, the patient recounted his recollection of his mother's smell to Freud. Mention of a temptation to touch his mother's underwear, led him to speak of revulsion at women's 'secretions'. Freud associates the Ratman's revolt against certain smells to his mother's 'abdominal affection' that resulted in a bad smell from her genitals and notes that the patient's mother herself had said that she stank unless she took regular baths, which she could not afford to do. We may also wonder here whether the Ratman's repulsion to women's smell was related, not to his actual experience of his mother's bad smell, but rather to his mother's narrative on that subject.

Generally, we may wonder how much the weight of olfactory references in the narrative of the care giver of infancy can impact the subject's unconscious strategy in dealing with the object of lack in the Other. In obsessional neurosis, for example, the subject's guesswork in relation to the Other's desire usually leads to a reductive approach, meaning that they reduce desire to an assumed demand of the Other, which they find easier to deal with. Evidently, generalisation and compartmentalisation are common strategies in the clinic of many cases of obsessional neurosis, where they are used as tools to deal with the lack inherent to castration. The obsessional's assertion that all women are such and such, or the so-called Madonna/whore complex, are examples of such an approach to the Other's desire.

In the Ratman's case, was the reference to smell in the mother's narrative treated literally as an indicator of social status (not being able to afford regular baths) or metaphorically as a generalised property associated with women and his lover(s), as in 'all women stink unless proven otherwise'? In Freud's interpretation of the Ratman's symptomology, the olfactory reference had found an expression in his arrangement (montage) of the drive.

According to Freud, grown-ups are more susceptible to sensations of smell than children. He acknowledges that such a trait can be found in both hysteria and obsessional neurosis and (as quoted above), he admits that humans have repressed pleasure from their atrophied sense of smell in the process of civilization and says this might have played a role in the genesis of neurosis. Here, we need to make a distinction between the effect of so-called Freudian 'organic repression' and cultural education on how olfaction is understood in psychoanalysis. A subject's disgust towards certain smells cannot simply be a result of cultivation. This is particularly evident in the clinic of perversion. The smell of bodily waste can be as sexually arousing to some people as an expensive fragrance to others. Freud was very clear on this in two letters to Wilhelm Fliess dated 11th January and 14th November 1897 when he had not yet abandoned the seduction theory. He suggested that disgust towards excrement and many other phenomena of disgust and shame were a phylogenetic consequence of the adoption by human beings of an upright posture. He linked shame to the visibility of sexual organs, due again to the upright posture, which he also took to be explanatory of the prestige accorded to vision as opposed to smell. We should note that what Freud is emphasising here is the 'organic' repression of the sense of smell and not the educational effect of civilisation. In a footnote to his *Three Essays on Sexuality*, Freud refers to the subject's choice of a fetish as linked to 'a coprophilic pleasure in smelling' which has been repressed. He considers hair and feet to be common fetish objects due to their strong smell. They have become fetishes as remainders of a loss: the loss of olfactory pleasure. In Freud's clinical observation, foot fetishists were only attracted to 'evil-smelling' feet (Freud, 1910, p. 155). He also associates fetishism with scoptophilia, an apparently tenuous connection, which demonstrates how our sexuality has a complicated structure and function unlike that of any other species on the planet. Such a conclusion shows us the interconnectivity of the ways of gaining pleasure in a human subject (the ways in which our body enjoys itself). The smell fetish, from perfume to the odour of sweat, underwear or excrement (coprophilia), can be considered a different category from fetishism based on body parts or clothes.

In 1910, Freud came back to olfaction in his 'Contributions to the Psychology of Love' by way of a reference to coprophilia. He believed that some components of the 'sexual drive' (the *Standard Edition* translates 'Trieb' as 'instinct', which I correct to the more accurate 'drive') are suppressed or find another functionality, which he labelled 'coprophilic drive components'. They were, according to Freud, 'incompatible with our aesthetic standards of culture, probably since, as a result of our adopting an erect gait, we raised out organ of smell from the ground.' (Freud, 1910, p. 188) However, he adds that the change of posture has not prevented the human subject from obtaining erotic excitation from this drive component. Furthermore, he adds that the anatomical position of the excremental function, proximal to the genitals, plays a role in such excitation.

Freud's remarks are part of his broader argument that the demands of the sexual drive cannot be accommodated by human civilization. His suggestion that human discontent in recent ages (see the title of his later work, 'Civilisation and its Discontents' (Freud, 1926)) has to do with restrictions on our use of the sense of smell is based on evolutionary assumptions and obvious points about human anatomy, but it nevertheless amounts to a quite radical comment on the function of olfaction. Freud put loss of pleasure in smell at the root of man's neurosis and unhappiness in civilization. The question, which we should then ask is: how does such a loss find a new life in the subject's civilised being?

The response of the first generation of post-Freudian psychoanalysts to his question was that the sense of smell is connected with anal eroticism. Ferenczi, for instance, follows the classic interpretative linkage between dirt, money and anal eroticism – he connects defecation with interest in money.

He says that children renounce their initial keen interest in their own faeces (their first toy) due mainly to its smell, although they may continue to derive tactile enjoyment from touching mud in the street or similar objects as a symbolic replacement for the 'disgusting, smelly' faeces. For Ferenczi, the destiny of pleasure in foul-smells, after its suppression, is sublimation and reaction formation as interest in perfume or the smell of cleanliness. Ferenczi suggested that the Latin expression 'Pecunia non olet' (money doesn't smell) conceals the truth of its unnegated form, 'Pecunia olet' (money smells), which confirms the equation between money and excrement. He equates anal eroticism with interest in money and concludes that the love of odours is the same as the love of money, offering clinical examples of patients who were obsessed with the smell of their own or others' bodies to support his argument. To him, smell in a patient's narrative indicates a specific unconscious meaning. In one case cited by Ferenczi, a young obsessional man confirmed that his marriage was motivated by interest in money rather than love by reporting that he almost called the marriage off after noting an unpleasant smell from his fiancé's mouth when he kissed her. Ferenczi's idea is that the money-excrement-smell association aroused the young man's guilt over his self-seeking behaviour (Ferenczi, 1994, p. 362).

In his book, *Thalassa* Ferenczi suggests that the eye has taken over the role of the nose as the dominant sense due to man's shift to an upright posture but he also suggests that smell remains the 'biological prototype of thought'. The sense of smell has a much lesser role in detecting food and a sexual mate for humans than for other animals, but it still retains a significant role in the 'intellectualised' sexuality of human beings. Ferenczi notes that, as the cerebral hemispheres developed in the course of human evolution, the rhinencephalon (the main olfactory part of the forebrain, which he distinguishes from the cerebrum) shrank as upright posture gave priority to the eyes over the organ of smell, the nose. An analogy between the role of the sense of smell in animals and thought (governed by the cerebrum) in man as the principal means of orientation in reality leads Ferenczi to say that 'the functioning of the organ of smell exhibits an analogy with thought which is so intensive and complete that smell may properly be considered the biological prototype of thought' (Ferenczi, 1968, p. 71).

Clearly, Ferenczi was taking up Freud's thoughts about the organic aspect of the sense of smell and human evolution. In his records of a couple of other clinical cases, Ferenczi highlights the presence of smell in the subject's narrative as describing a paranoid position towards others. One patient purposely did not wash her body so that other people would be repelled by the bad smell. Her argument was that she wanted to scare them off, so that they would not fall victim to her hatred. Ferenczi intuited that her rage and hatred were due to trauma at the hands of a cruel mother. A foul-smelling body was the patient's defence against the intrusions of other people. So, she was filtering an assumed aggressiveness of others towards her being (and her body) and

Ferenczi shows that an olfactory memory had helped her to reconstruct the traumatising history.

In a case from my own practice, a patient was taken to the psychiatric hospital following a psychotic breakdown in which he had covered himself with his own faeces. When found in that condition, before being sectioned, he repeatedly shouted 'I stink', as if in order to discourage his relocation to the hospital. He had persecutory hallucinations, where his mother was running after him in order to catch him. He described his mother as a 'cruel, selfish, rotten woman' who had repeatedly beaten and verbally abused him. When he was five years old she had even attempted to kill him and his younger brother by trying to choke them, but was prevented by another family member. His mother eventually took her own life and her body was discovered by the patient a few days after her death in the garage of the family house. His father had left the family soon after the death of the patient's brother. The patient's mother had described him as a 'filthy man'.

After being discharged from the psychiatric hospital, the patient refused to take baths and his family was concerned for both his physical and mental health. Prior to his psychotic breakdown, he had been obsessed with personal hygiene and particularly with preventing any body odours. Excessive use of Eau de Cologne had caused him to develop a reactive airways condition and he said in an interview with a psychiatric nurse that he was unable to tolerate the smell of his own skin. Up until the triggering of his psychosis, his lifestyle had focused on bodily hygiene and maintaining a space around him, apparently to prevent any identification with his parents – his mother whose body was 'rotten' (literally, after she had lain dead for days after her suicide) and his father, whose presence in his mother's narrative was highlighted by the olfactory signifier 'filthy'. He was equating the smell of his own body with that of his parents – his mother who was found 'rotten' and the father who was 'filth' in his mother's narrative. By perfuming his skin, he not only covered his own body odour, but also created a border between his own body and the bodies of both of his parents. Why then, at the time of his psychotic breakdown, had he covered himself with faeces and suffered hallucinations of being pursued by his mother? As became more evident in the course of the talking therapy, which followed his discharge from the hospital, his mother had also been obsessed with the suppression of bad smells. She cleaned the house to excess and washed her children for hours in the bath tub, leaving them for a long time in a hot bath to 'soak' before washing them until their skin became red and irritable. As an adult, the patient had suffered from nightmares, in which he was trapped in the bathroom.

In the patient's own construction, covering himself with faeces was a way of punishing his mother. 'Smell' for him was much more than the literal object of olfaction; it was a signifier punctuating the subject's way of separating his being from the Other – a way of creating a border. In other words, smell was not simply the odour of a perfume or a stench. It had an all-pervasive presence beyond sensory stimuli that generate pleasure or disgust and was not reducible to individual or social identity. The strong olfactory reference, 'stink', was disconnected from the usual sense of the word. Having been overwhelmed by his mother's cleanliness obsession, and literally smothered by her (her attempt to kill him), his perfume obsession in later life led to a respiratory condition, inviting us to reflect on the question (already touched on) of breathing as a principle condition for smelling. We will return to this point later in the chapter on breathing and smell.

Some Concluding Remarks

We rely on olfactory memories, which evoke intense emotional responses in us. We experience and express certain emotions and feelings when we sense certain odours, from our own or others' bodies, or in the environment or as a companion to oral satisfaction. Odour remains a powerful tool for detecting threats to our health or safety. In particular, it helps us to recognise and identify rotten food or bodily illness. More than all that, smell has a life in language for a speaking being. Certain olfactory references in language (the 'smelly' words) have only to be uttered in order to provoke a feeling or even a bodily sensation, or they may be avoided as forbidden terms. In many cultures, to comment on someone else's smell (if not agreeable) is a taboo. In the case of perfume, on the contrary, it may be *de rigueur* to comment (favourably) on their fragrance.

What, then, is smell once we have agreed that it cannot be reduced to qualitative meanings such as fragrance or stench, and that it is not definable simply based on its functionality and the purposes (scientific and other) that it serves today?

Human olfaction may have lost its absolute primacy among the senses, for humans as compared to other animals, in the course of evolution, but the decisive role of this sense in our formation as a human being remains undeniable. Olfaction is not only the most primitive of the senses; it is also the most intimate when we reflect on the infant's social bonding with the care giver. Earlier in this chapter, I discussed the relationship of the child (the subject to be) to the mother's smell and their own smell and considered olfaction (a marker of the real) as a sense that serves a central role in alienation and separation from the Other. I will come back to and elaborate this point through clinical examples in the next chapter, which considers the status of smell as a 'lost' sense.

We may now wonder about the mother's relation to olfaction at the level of first bonding. Just as new-borns and young children are able to recognise the smell of their mother, the mother, for her part, can usually identify and enjoy the odour of her young child. Sniffing the child is common practice among mothers, justified for various reasons, from checking on the general state of health of the baby to gaining a sense of emotional connection or simply enjoying the smell of new life. Close bonding between parent and child relies heavily on such olfactory practice. There are, however, instances when a mother shows a strong repugnance for the smell of her infant, notably when mothers suffer from post-partum depression or a triggered psychosis after giving birth. Olfactory aversion can also be a transient condition, experienced by some pregnant women or immediately after giving birth. These experiences can occasionally verge on the uncanny. A patient of mine reported an overwhelming sense of anxiety during the early weeks of pregnancy (first trimester), when she had become oversensitive towards certain smells, particularly the smell of her own body. Her anxious state led to obsessional rituals of cleaning and using strong odorants to cover the natural odour of her body. She gradually felt relieved from her anxiety over her own smell towards the end of her pregnancy. She was surprised by the psychical reaction (oversensitivity towards her body odour) that came with the hormonal change in early pregnancy. Up until that moment in her life she had never experienced any form of obsession associated with smell. After giving birth, she suffered from post-partum depression and had an acute distaste for the smell of her baby. The effect of this olfactory discomfort on mother-child bonding was manifested when the child stopped being breast fed and refused to take its mother's milk from a bottle. Can smell in this case be simply defined as a stimulus for the chemoreceptors or did it function as a silent but powerful narrative at the level of first bonding between mother and child? I will say more about this in the last chapter of the book, but we should already raise the question why, for a speaking being, a sense such as olfaction cannot remain at the merely perceptual level.

Let us consider another aspect of the powerful role of smell in the earliest social bond of the subject; a bond, which leaves a mark on the birth of the subject of the unconscious.

In cases where olfactory aversion is presented as the main clinical feature that spurs a subject to demand analysis, odour takes a central role in punctuating the distance between the subject and the Other. I will look at this question in detail in Chapter 3 with reference to the work of Francoise Dolto.

If a mother cannot smell her child, what happens to mother-child bonding? What we find is that the olfactory reference is, as it were, omnipresent in its absence and still serves a particular purpose at the level of bonding. Consider the case of a mother who suffered from anosmia after recovering from Covid-19. She was breast feeding her two-week-old daughter when she caught the illness. She recovered from most of the symptoms after a couple of weeks, but remained unable to smell her child for around six months. She was upset for practical reasons (the anosmia made child care difficult) and concerned about how her own bodily and milk smells were perceived by the child. She had devised some practical ways to mend the situation, but it was apparent that the 'perceptual ignorance' arising from loss of such an instinctive, primitive sense had affected her mental life. Having to ask her partner to sniff the infant in order to check on its physical condition was a source of much distress to her. In her analysis, she was fixated on the anosmia in respect of her baby instead of paying attention to other aspects of their bonding: her infant's reactions and responses, contestations, contentment or discontent in the mother-child relationship. It is certainly true that other forms of sensory deprivation on the side of mother can disrupt the bonding process, by provoking anxiety on the part of the mother. However, the source of anxiety in the present case was not simply the mother's preoccupation with her inability to carry out her tasks and duties; it was a disturbing silence of the olfactory narrative, which not only punctuates and regulates a primary social bond, reassuring both sides in the exchange of care and love between them (albeit mixed with ambivalent feelings of frustration, anger, etc.), but also provides a context for the necessary processes of alienation and separation on both sides. Anosmia on the side of the mother has the potential to hinder the creation of a space where the child can choose whether to take up a position towards the mother's deprivation, and whether to break out of the maternal, fusional nest. How can such hindrance occur? In the present case, the mother was focused on keeping the rituals/chores of child care in place in order to keep her child healthy and secure its needs, while dealing with her own frustration at the loss of a fundamental, instinctive and pleasurable sense. Her immersion in these tasks was covering over a deprivation in the Real and thereby making it harder for the child-subject to respond to that deprivation in whatever way it chose. The mother was so distraught by her inability to smell that all of her active strategies were focused on minimising what she took to be the negative impact of this olfactory failure on the infant. So, she was giving a *physiological* status to the olfaction rather than leaving a space at the symbolic level, which she might have done, for example, by talking more about her temporary inability to smell her baby. Her eagerness to mend the shortcoming tended to give olfaction a literal, practical meaning, ignoring its symbolic dimension, which was, in fact, the dimension where the problem could be better dealt with. The result, on the side of the child, was an indifference towards the mother, manifested by lack of eye contact, screaming and an unwillingness to frame words in the second year of life.

In both of these last two cases – the first of traumatism from exposure to unknown smells and the second of anosmia – difficulties in mother-child bonding arise from abnormalities in relation to olfaction and we see the profound impact of smell on the subject's consciousness (awareness of self) and on their exercise of agency when positioning themselves in relation to the Other of body and language.

The Covid pandemic left many people with long- or short-term anosmia or parosmia (altered sense of smell) and lack of socialisation with other people during lockdown caused many people to experience over- or under-sensitivity to certain odours. The Covid experience shows us once more the extent to which olfaction is a social sense and the olfaction-related impact of Covid on mental health (particularly in younger generations) can be imagined.

In my own clinical experience, I heard different narratives around social change at the level of our experience of olfaction due to Covid. Some people were pleased at not having to be exposed to the smell of other humans or certain other odours, while others indulged and embraced olfactory pleasure through greater use of perfumes or air fresheners. There were also cases of olfactory obsession which found relief in the lack of exposure to smells during lockdown or in their own anosmia after contracting the virus. One patient with a prolonged anosmia followed by parosmia over a period of a year reported of numerous 'smelly' dreams (a simple demonstration of Freud's doctrine that dreams are wish fulfilments). When the content of the dreams and the relation of the subject to the relevant odours were explored, it became clear that smells in the dreams served as temporal and spatial metrics. The subject reported and described the odour of particular seasons and familiar places or of objects, which were used seasonally instead of describing actual foods, places or objects, and it was clear that the patient's symptom of moving places and jobs was circumscribed in this way. The olfactory references to his symptom in his dreams when he was unable to smell opened up a space for reconsidering his position towards his symptom, creating a narrative where he was able to see the repetition of a symptomatic pattern.

When we lose someone close to us, it is common practice to smell their personal belongings in order to remember them or feel close to them. The effect of such a practice cannot be replaced by watching a video, listening to their recorded voice or looking at a photograph. What does this tell us about our relationship to smell? In the next few chapters, I will attempt to explore in more depth the question that was raised in the title of this chapter: *what is smell?* I will start by asking whether the sense of smell is really a 'lost sense' and how that might be visible in the psychoanalytical and socio-cultural literature of the past and the present.

Bibliography

Classon, C. (1994). The Aromas of Antiquity. pp. 13– 25. In: *Aroma: The Cultural History of Smell*, (eds). London: Routledge

De Montaigne, M. (2003). On Smells. pp. 352–354. In: *Michel De Montaigne: The Complete Essays*, M.A. Screech (Trans). London: Penguine Group

Ferenczi, S. (1994). *Further Contributions to the Theory and Technique of Psychoanalysis. Suttie, J. 1 & Others*. (Trans). London: Karnac

Ferencz, S. (1968). *Thalassa: A Theory of Genitality*. Bunker, H. A. (Trans). New York: *W.W. Norton & Company. Inc*

Freud, S. (1893–1895). Case Histories. pp. 19–182. In: *J. Strachey, ed. The Standard Edition of the Complete Psychological Works of Sigmund Freud, Vol 2*. London: Vintage, 2001

Freud, S. (1909). Two Case Histories: "Little Hans and The Rat Man". pp. 3–149 In: *J. Strachey, ed. The Standard Edition of the Complete Psychological Works of Sigmund Freud, Vol X*. London: Vintage, 2001

Freud, S. (1910). On the Universal Tendency to Debasement in the Sphere of Love (Contributions To The Psychology Of Love II) (1912). pp. 177–191 In: J. Strachey, ed. *The Standard Edition of the Complete Psychological Works of Sigmund Freud*, Vol XI. London: Vintage, 2001

Freud, S. (1920). Beyond the Pleasure Principle, pp. 7–64. In: J. Strachey, ed. *The Standard Edition of the Complete Psychological Works of Sigmund Freud*, Vol. XVIII. London: Vintage

Freud, S. (1926). Civilization and Its Discontents, pp. 57–147. In: J. Strachey, ed. *The Standard Edition of the Complete Psychological Works of Sigmund Freud*, Vol. XXI. London: Vintage

Jazani, B. (2021). *Lacan, Mortality, Life and Language: Clinical and Cultural Explorations*. London: Routledge.

Le Guerer, A. (1992). *Scent: The Mysterious and Essential Powers of Smell*. Miller, R. (Trans). New York: Turtle Bay Books

Rousseau, J. J. (1991). *Emile; Or On Education*. London: Penguin

Chapter 3

A Lost Sense?

Introduction

Olfaction, as the most primitive of all the senses, is a sense that is culture-bound. Philosophy or cognitive science may offer sophisticated theorisations of the sense of smell, but the power of odours is experienced by a subject in a way that no knowledge can teach. The involuntary, instant temporal and spatial transportation provoked by a specific scent traverses any conventional borders and boundaries. Baudelaire, in his poem *The Perfume Flask* (*Le Flacon*), cites olfaction as the most powerful reminder of the past, of life and of mortality. His poem makes death, decay and the return to life present to the reader through rich olfactory language. This poem can be read as an ontological approach to smell, making a familiar bodily experience meaningful through the language of poetry. Particular features of odour and its effect on the subject are brought out by the poet with consummate skill. The visceral sense of the past that bursts forth when an 'antique phial' is opened and sniffed – not so much the subject's own forgotten memories of the past as the smell of a past lived by others – shows well how the power of scents cannot be contained. Smell travels above the usual, conventional passage of time. It flies away and comes back, penetrating and filling every crack and cranny. In a word, smell is immortal. When Baudelaire writes that the poet is dead, thrown away, forgotten and abject – like a fragrance in an old phial – he becomes the recorded memory of a time of pestilence, 'the coffin of pestilence', like a smell trapped in a flask that works as a reminder of death. Will he come back to life when a curious soul from the future finds the phial and repeats his experiment?

Smell is the most neglected of the five senses in psychoanalytic writing, which is surprising in view of the elaborated treatments of olfaction in literature and the history of medicine. The sense of smell is a frequent reference in poetry (the language of metaphors), where odours evoke lust and nostalgia in a subject, and odours and respiration have been markers of health and the treatment of disease from ancient medicine to the most recent research on the use of trained dogs to identify the smell of a body infected with COVID-19.

DOI: 10.4324/9781003485322-3

At the level of language, olfaction signifies an intuitive detection or suspicion (to be 'on the scent' of some hidden fact or mystery) in a way that parallels the linkage of sight and human wisdom (the word 'insight', from Middle English, means inner sight or wisdom). Although recent western philosophical approaches to the concept of consciousness emphasise visuality (looking and observing), more ancient sources give at least equal place to olfaction. Mackenzie's dictionary of Pahlavi (a middle Persian language) tells us that the term which is used for 'smell' as a bodily sense also signifies 'meaning/sense', 'understanding' as well as 'consciousness' (Mackenzie, 1971). With such a nature and function, olfaction seems an excellent starting point for the psychoanalytic approach to the question of truth. Resistance to cognitive understanding and to what appears 'obvious' are common to the analytic discourse and olfactory experience. The analytic discourse, being concerned with the actual causes of certain subjective effects, is a journey rather than an end product. During such a journey, the impacts are not measurable but evident in an individual's life. Such a take on analytic practice makes the question of regulation a complicated matter. Smell, not necessarily as an intuitive value but rather as a narrative of the body, has to do with suspecting and detecting a truth, in which role it has occupied an important place in language for thousands of years. In psychoanalysis, subjective truth is unseen but present, not immediately noticeable as it appears in the gaps of speech (Jacques Lacan uses the resonant French word 'béance' (Lacan, 1953–1954)), which originally means something like 'lying open', to express this. The subject is unaware of it until it is accessed as an unconscious knowledge, which contains a kernel of truth. Perhaps we can call this moment of awareness 'analytic consciousness'. It is the being or becoming aware of our subjectivity, which cannot be fully defined by any neurobiological understanding of what we are as speaking beings.

The Smell of Affliction

The doctor's sense of smell was once an important means of detecting disease. Before the visual examination on an afflicted body, before listening to the sounds of the body, and certainly long before the privileged access and detailed observation made possible by today's high-tech scanning, the sense of smell of an experienced physician was a reliable tool for diagnosis. The olfactory sense was not merely a sense. It was a guiding tool for verifying a diagnosis or assessing a prognosis. Bad odour was a sign of poor health or even of imminent death and a change in the usual smell of the body signalled the loss of bodily homeostasis. While the smell of the body was a signifier of the state of health, the smell of the air around the body was seen as a cause of illness or even as the bearer of deadly diseases, most notably plague. Our ancestors attempted to purify polluted air by fire and the burning of incense (huge fires were kept alight in open spaces in ancient Athens when the city was afflicted by plague). Annick Le Guerer, in her book on scent looks at the origins of the idea that odours could cleanse and purify corrupted air, noting the belief of the ancient Egyptians that certain odours were a medium for communication between humans and gods, and that they could even be employed to calm divine anger directed at humans. The Greek botanist Theophrastus believed that pleasant odours had curative power because of their fiery, hot and dry nature. The burning of perfume as a treatment for illness has been practised since ancient times and was supposed by physicians (including Hippocrates) to purify the air (Le Guerer, 1992).

The emphasis in Greek and Roman medicine was on the smell of decay as both a threat to health and a sign of illness, and on the use of scents to banish that smell and thereby prevent or overcome illness. Not only did bodily odours signify the nature and prognosis of a particular condition of the body, but smell had a role both as the cause of illness and as an effective remedy. Corrupted air was supposed to cause life-threatening illnesses, plague and pestilence and the burning of aromatic scents was supposed to act as a remedy.

Through the Middle Ages, more efficient methods were found for extracting and preserving the scents of herbs, flowers and aromatic substances and the extracts were put to other uses in addition to the treatment of physical illness. The Persian philosopher and physician Avicenna introduced a method for distilling the essential oil from roses, and rose oil and rosewater were taken to be powerful remedies for psychological ailments as well as having a curative effect on digestive disorders. States of fright and despair were treated by the use of perfumes. The use of scents to treat mental suffering is, of course, still common in alternative medicine around the world today.

The best-known use of aromas in preventive medicine was surely during the Black Death – the bubonic plague pandemic of the 14th century – when the principal medical advice was to inhale various aromatics, differing between the hot and cold seasons, in order to maintain a balance between body and air. Hot smelling aromas were prescribed for winter and cold aromas for summer. By the 17th century, the use of strong smells to combat dangerous diseases gave way to the use of less strong but highly toxic chemicals as disinfectants. But the use of perfume remained an important part of disinfection until the late 18th century. The overall trend was from suppressing fetid odours to the creation of antidotes against their effects (Le Guerer, 1992, p. 229).

As was briefly mentioned in the previous chapter, it is important to consider how the treatment of odours as a source of infection was related to the act of breathing as the principal way in which the body became infected. There will be more to say about this in the later chapter on breathing and olfaction.

The use of spices, either swallowed or inhaled during the cold season, was believed to open the pores of the skin, creating and maintaining a balance between the body and the surrounding air. However, the pores of the skin were also believed to be a path of access into the body for infection. So regular baths, which could open the pores, was strongly discouraged during times of plague. Preference was given to regular changes of clothes and covering the skin and hair with scented unguents. So, the olfactory sense was given pride of place in preventive medicine, and the taking of baths was viewed as dangerous in the extreme. The marker and gauge of a medicine's efficacy in improving a patient's condition was its smell and if a remedy was lacking an aroma, it was less trusted as a cure.

The close linkage between odours and health created a primitive but highly elaborate hierarchy of good and bad smells in the Ancient World and until the 18th century, when the growth of urban life was accompanied by a contrary drive towards deodorisation as the focus of public hygiene. The psychological effect of this huge olfactory reference in past centuries is highly thought-provoking. We can ask how the categorising system of pleasant and unpleasant smells, stemming from Aristotle's theorisation of odours, with its many implications that appear so absurd to us today (including the preference for smelly skin, doused with unguents, as opposed to washing away any residue of smell on the skin by the use of running water), marked the subject as a sexed and social being. How did the cultural change in respect of personal hygiene affect a subject's relation to his or her body through the Middle Ages and Renaissance?

The role of odours and the sense of smell in middle-eastern and oriental medicine in past centuries was similar to that in western medicine. Touching and smelling were believed to be the two principal modes of contamination. In his book on Persian medical history, Cyril Elgood notes that in Persian mythology the origin of medicine as a science is ascribed to Jamshid, an ancient king of Iran. This is made plain in the *Book of Kings*, the epic of Persian history written by Ferdowsi, a poet of the 9th century, in which the art of healing the sick, the means of health and care, the discovery of the causes of illnesses and also the discovery of alcohol were all innovations made under Jamshid's rule (Elgood, 2010).

The Babylonians and Assyrians had believed that health and disease were in the hands of the gods and that cure had to be sought through prayer and magic spells, i.e., through patience and intercession. In Zoroastrianism, in texts that we can still read today, smell is treated in the context of medicine and hygiene, and perfume is used for purification as well as for medical remedies. Cold, heat, hunger, thirst, anxiety and old age were the possible causes of natural diseases, and stench and dirt were considered to be the cause of infectious diseases and of epidemics. Putrefaction was a process, which defiled the four natural elements of water, air, earth and fire. The basic system for controlling public health and hygiene was to avoid the touch and smell of dirt and decay. Animal and human waste must not be thrown into water; but fire, as a sacred element, could not be used as a steriliser, although the burning of incense to produce purifying smoke and odour was countenanced. The bodies of the dead were taken to a 'Tower of Silence' rather than being buried in the ground. The body of a person whose death was imminent was disinfected before his or her actual death. Those who took part in burial ceremonies were required to bathe afterwards. The heat and light of the sun were used for cleansing and disinfection. An ancient collection of texts, the *Vendidad*, which is a part of *Avesta*, the religious book of Zoroastrianism, describes in detail the cleansing process for those who had attended a funeral, including disinfection and washing of their body and clothes, and anointment with herbal perfumes. According to the *Vendidad*, the use of perfume was not intended to cover a bad smell but to complete the cleansing process. However, the overall ritual was meant to prevent the spread of sickness and can also be read as a way of transforming the smell of death and decay associated with the deceased into a pleasant odour of life for the living. In this context, the smell of perfume, as a sign of life, can be seen as a marking factor for a new stage in the process of mourning. One factor to consider here would be a form of learning by conditioning – the association of certain pleasant odours with grief or mourning. More generally, the use of pleasant scents as an accompaniment to religious rituals can change the meaning of pleasant smells for the participants in the ritual. This will be discussed in more depth further on (Horne, 2010).

Avicenna treated a range of nervous diseases and psychological conditions by prescribing aromatic herbal drugs, for either ingestion or inhalation. Regulations on the preparation of drugs, food and drink, as well as hygiene at the public baths, were part of the governing law in Avicenna's time. Drugstores, public eating places, slaughterhouses, bakeries and public baths were inspected regularly and were evaluated mainly by their smell. The drugstore owner was called 'Attar', which means 'dealer in perfumes', and some of the preparations he dealt in, made by doctors, were believed to have curative effects by their odour alone.

Aromas were also valued for their anaesthetic properties in the practice of surgery or dentistry. According to Herodotus, the Saka, an ancient nomadic people of Iranian origin, inhaled the smoke of burnt herbs to alleviate pain during the performance of medical operations. Intoxicants, from opium to much less powerful poppy and belladonna, were much used for anaesthesia and were often administered through respiration and smell. In the 10th century, in the countries of the Middle East narcosis was induced during painful medical procedures by means of a narcotic sponge placed under the nose of the patient. The technique was brought to Europe around the 13th century and was used in combination with wine to induce sleep. The constituents used on the sponge are recorded as 'seeds of mint, anemone and black henbane, euphorbia, Egyptian opium, tamarisk, expressed juice of jasmine and a kind of crocus', which were compressed, fermented, dried and burnt to produce a powder (Elgood, 2010, p. 284).

Philosophical Scents

The literature of antiquity is filled with evidence of the importance, which olfactory experience had for people in those times, not just in medicine but throughout society. Beyond their personal use, scents played an important role in major public events such as religious rituals and sports. Smell, in those days, was not a lost sense. The evolution of civilisation and of social and philosophical theories was indebted to thinking about the senses, including the sense of smell. In Homer's *Iliad* and *Odyssey*, which reflect pre-Socratic thinking, olfactory experience consists mainly of the smell of cooked food and burning incense. Treatment of sense perception, including the sense of smell, at that time was experimental and not rational: Pre-socratic thought on smell was not concerned with the hierarchy of senses to the extent that one finds in the theories of the senses of the classical period in Ancient Greece. According to Theophrastus, the Pre-socratic approach explained the five senses according to their similarities (Empedocles) or based on their differences (Anaxagoras'). Theophrastus reports that Empedocles attributed the phenomenon of olfaction to breathing, while Diogenes argued that smell was in the air itself (Baltussen, 2014).

Pliny the Elder, the Roman philosopher of the first century AD, wrote in his *Natural History* of the use of pleasant odours for practical purposes beyond personal or social pleasure. He describes how spatial and time metrics as well as weather forecasting and prediction of soil fertility could be based on olfactory perception. For instance, the intensity of a fragrance indicates the proximity to or distance from an odorous object. The smell of air or earth signified the fertility of soil after rain and sun, and different times of the day were indexed according to the smell of flowers. (Classon, 1994). The Stoic philosopher, Epictetus, believed that the sense of smell was one of the faculties of the soul. (Epictetus, 2022, discourses 2.10.21)

As discussed in the previous chapter on philosophical theorisations of smell and odours, smell has been given a middle position among the senses since Plato. Such rankings were based on the power of the perceptions that each sense generates and hence the sort of knowledge that a person can access from his or her being and environment via each sense. Plato, in the *Timaeus*, refers to the incomplete nature of odour (the object of olfaction), calling it 'half-formed' because odours occur as a result of a transformative process in a body or an object. So, smell, for Plato, has to do with change, where odours, pleasant or foul, are indicators of change. They reveal both the presence of the object, which is undergoing the change, and the change itself, which cannot be easily seen, let alone heard or felt through the tactile sense. Smell is a revealing element, which never deceives.

The Roman poet and philosopher, Lucretius, in his philosophical poem *On the Nature of Things,* took a different view. For Lucretius, odours have transient and short-lived qualities, which make olfaction less important for us than colour and sound. He compares smell with the human soul: both can last only a little time outside the body and have a fading quality. Although smells have a transient quality, their impact can be immense and profound. Lucretius's treatment of odours is more concerned with cause than with effect and he points out that odours can affect different people differently.

Generally, philosophy has often focused on the question of the pleasure that is obtained through the senses, including the sense of smell. The status of olfactory experience is ambiguous in this respect. On the Platonic approach those sensory experiences are pleasurable, which can elevate the soul, whereas sensations (notably libidinal sensations) which are not driven by human wisdom are destructive to the subject's being. In this anti-hedonistic approach, pleasure has to be shaped and directed by the intellect in order to be compatible with virtue. The sense of smell has dual status: when olfactory sensation elevates the soul and promotes contemplation, it is akin to platonic pleasure, and hence essentially human, but when it provokes lust and sexual indulgence, its status is animalistic and non-virtuous. Problems arise when the boundary between the two statuses becomes blurred; if, for example, a smell that is usually animalistic somehow leads to intellectual fruition, or a refined, noble scent, which may even be considered sacred, arouses sexual temptation. So, the status of olfactory experience is closely bound up with culture and transcends brute sensory experience. Christianity, at its dawn, condemned both personal and social use of scents (on the body and at social or religious events). Indeed, the new religion viewed any sensual pleasure with disfavour until the 6th century when the use of incense became part of Christian ritual (Atchely, 2015), and odours and perfume became associated with holiness. Odour was transformed from a signifier of sin into a signifier of righteousness, and sweet odour became both a marker of divine presence and a sign of virtue.

As can be seen, philosophy takes odours to be a volatile and unstable category, which certainly corresponds to the actual nature of odours as theorised by science. The subject is brought to a halt upon sensing a particular odour, which serves as a marker of the Real in the Lacanian sense. The unexpected, eruptive encounter introduces the subject to an olfactory narrative happening in real time and this narrative, which is located outside language, testifies to a dimension of the subject's being, which has remained outside any symbolisation after the acquisition of language, what Lacan calls the 'real body'. Topologically, therefore, the direction of olfactory language does not follow or move in parallel with the subject's speech but crosses and cuts through the path that words usually follow in our everyday conversations. This is particularly evident when the olfactory sensation and the excitation gained through it, at the level of the body, captures and indexes what remains lost in spoken words. That is to say that olfaction is both a real experience and a narrative, simultaneously offering the subject an experience of the Real and indexing the register of the Real.

While the treatment of vision in philosophy is very different from its treatment in psychoanalysis, the approach to olfaction in some philosophical literatures (particularly in non-western traditions) comes quite close to the psychoanalytical approach to human subjectivity. In Persian thought, the term used for smell and smelling is 'boy' which also means consciousness. (Gignoux, 2001, p. 22). Zadespram, a Zoroastrian scholar of the 9th and 10th centuries, writes in in chapters 29 and 30 of his work, *The Anthology (Vizīdagīhā ī Zādspram)*, that the human being is composed of four formations: body ('tan'), life breath/vital soul ('jaan'/'gyan'), knowledge ('danishn') and the mental soul or mind ('ruwan'). According to Zadespram, the mental soul rules and controls the body and is superior to the vital soul ('gyan'). An analysis of *The Anthology* by Philippe Gignoux argues that Zadespram's definition of the human being echoes Greek philosophy and the medical thinking of Galen and Hippocrates, but that Zadespram's concept of the mind is original. The Persian author finds three different agencies in the mind: one which remains in the body (the corporeal mind), another that leaves the body (the external mind) and a third, which is immortal ('menog'). From an ontological perspective the mind is the same as 'menog', which many readers of the original text have wrongly interpreted as equivalent to wisdom. Zadespram believes that the mind leaves the body during sleep and returns to it upon waking. Zadespram takes 'boy' (consciousness/smell) to be the messenger between the mind and the vital soul in the body at times when the body is asleep. 'Boy' receives information from the mind and transmits it to the vital soul. It is the subject's realisation of their being inside and outside the mortal body, and Gignoux compares this idea with the psychoanalytic theory of the unconscious and the dream work. Smell is separate from and superior to the other senses because it acts as a messenger between two agencies: the immortal unconscious mind and the mortal bodily mind. Smell in this Zoroastrian theory is not merely a bodily sense but is the crux of what makes the human being. So, smell is a lost sense to the extent that it ceases to be a corporeal, perceptive sense, but it finds a new and vigorous role in language. The Pahlavi language of ancient Persia, in which *The Anthology* was written used olfactory references to designate subjective agency.

'Smelly' Literature

The links between olfaction and sexual desire are highlighted in poetry (that of Baudelaire and many others) and in religious precepts that prohibit the use of perfume in order to discourage sexual temptation. The notion that scents act as a pheromone or aphrodisiac for humans as much as for animals has made a fortune for the makers and purveyors of perfume, based on the simple idea that wearing a perfume with a specific odour can sexually attract and seduce others or boost sexual desire and potency. Although to date there is no strong physiological evidence to back up such a belief, 'aphrodisiac', 'pheromone' and similar words are popular with perfume marketeers, illustrating yet again how our submission to the law of language has changed the economy of our enjoyment. A pheromone is a chemical that is excreted or secreted from the body of an animal and that has an effect on other animals of the same species. Such chemicals are used mainly as a medium for communication, mating and other survival-related functions. 'Pheromone' has a Greek etymology consisting of the verbs 'pherein' and 'horman', meaning, respectively, 'to carry' and 'to impel'. Essentially, it is a hormone that acts between two or more bodies instead of acting inside a single body. Pheromones are detected in an olfactory membrane or by the vomeronasal organ, which exists mainly in vertebrates and is most prominent in humans at the embryonic stage (the presence of the organ in humans was discovered by Ludwig Lewin Jacobson in 1809, hence its alternative title, 'Jacobson's organ') (Annick Le Guerer, 1992).

Pop psychology and perfume marketing can make links between physiological findings about chemoreceptors in human beings, on the one hand, and behavioural patterns or personal taste on the other, and such analysis may offer some insights into the role of olfaction in the reality of everyday life. But in the psychoanalytic reading of sexual attraction and excitation, a subject does not need Jacobson's organ in order to feel sexually aroused or excited by a certain odour. The fact that a subject feels such excitement after sensing a particular scent can potentially say something about the subjective arrangement of the drive or what Lacan calls the 'montage of the drive' (Lacan, 1963–1964). This is where the life of a scent at the level of a sensual, bodily experience is extracted into language and then returns to the body, but not necessarily with the same quality or quantity of excitation. Language kills the immediacy and primacy of the olfactory excitation but it also gives it another form of life. This can even happen without the actual presence of the olfactory object – the smell. The effect on the subject can be produced by words alone. A person can, for example, have a pleasant or unpleasant response at the level of his feelings or as a bodily excitation upon reading or listening to a text or a narrative with olfactory references. There will be more to say about this in the chapter on the olfactory drive.

Smell is anything but a lost experience in philosophical and literary texts, which handle olfactory experience in all of its manifold aspects: the metaphorical language of emotions and affects; a sense concerned with social morality; in terms of sexual temptation and pleasure or of subjectivity and otherness; and with respect to the remembering or forgetting of the past (including our temporal and spatial awareness).

In this short treatise, entitled Khosrow and Ridag, a young, well-educated nobleman called Ridag responds to the questions of King Khosrow, who ruled Persia in the 7th century AD, about different sources of pleasure, including food, wine, music, women, horse-riding and smell. The King asks Ridag which plant has the best fragrance. Ridag replies that it is jasmin because the smell of jasmin is the favourite smell of the gods. The conversations between the King and his subject continue and associations are made between each group of society and the odour of a particular flower or plant, native to the Persian Empire at that time. Olfactory references are used as a sophisticated way of describing different formations in society – social classes, gender and identity, human characteristics and morality.

The treatise is an attempt to distinguish different sources of enjoyment, gained from the drives: scopic (visuality, emphasising the aesthetic aspect of one's surroundings), anal (education and cleanness), oral (food and drink, particularly wine), invocatory (music), and, above all, olfactory (fragrance). Smell is a prime marker in making the distinctions and it is interesting to see the logic at work in linking fragrances to social formations or conditions. The smell of jasmine has the first rank as coming from the gods; a prince smells like Smilax; people of noble ancestry have the smell of Ketaki; youth smells of narcissus; friendship has the odour of a red wallflower or Madonna lily; an unattached woman who is not a prostitute smells like a yellow wallflower; religious authorities (judges) smell like camphor; children smell like white star jasmine; a mother smells of mugwort and a father smells of white viper's buglos; young girls smell like violet; loved ones smell like basilic perfume; wealth smells like water lilies; medicine has the odour of marjoram; sick people smell like crambe maritima; couples smell of lemon balm; fame smells of camomile; an old woman smells like sweet-brier; and freedom is associated with the smell of Breckland thyme (Azarnouche, 2013).

The book of Arda Wiraf (or Arda Wiraz in Middle Persian), a text written in Pahlavi language, is a story of a journey of a devoted Zoroastrian, Arda Wiraf, to the next world. He takes this journey in order to prove the truthfulness of Zoroastrian belief. He drinks wine and henbane and it was the 'sweet smelling' scent, which facilitates his journey up to the sky. For his journey, which lasts for seven days, his body is washed and perfumed. Upon his arrival, he asked for good food and water whose quality were measured by their good smell. Moreover, during his journey he was shown the paradise and hell once again being distinguished by their smell. The joy and happiness in paradise were described to have 'sweet smell' (sweet smelling flowers), while the hell was recognised by the stench. The hell was referred to as a place of ugliness, filth, foul smell, rotten and stinky. The stench of hell was so powerful that could cause tremble and fainting in a subject. Moreover, the stench was a way to punish a sinner (Wahman, 2018).

A detailed collection of Zoroastrian cosmogony and cosmography, the *Bundahishn* or *Book of Primal Creation*, rewritten in the Pahlavi language around the 8th and 9th centuries based on a much older version in the Avestan language, has a section entitled 'On the Nature of Plants', which discusses the creation and classification of plants (Bahar, 2009). Plants are grouped into seventeen categories based on their use and function in everyday life. Four types of plants are identified by their pleasant odours: all good-smelling plants; flowers (blossoms with a pleasant smell); saplings that produce blossom or fruit; and plants with fragrant skin or roots. Plants and their odours are then closely linked to the Zoroastrian calendar (in use since the Achaemenid empire in the 5th century BC), which has 30-day months, where each day bears the name of a divinity or element. Four days are dedicated to Ahura Mazda, the creator and lord of wisdom; five days to (respectively) Fire, Water,

Sun, Moon and the Origin; one day to the soul of Ox (representing the creation of all animals), one day to Mithra (divinity of light and oath), two days to
the Yazatas of conscience and justice (Srosh and Rashnu), four days to Frava-
har (spirit of an individual), Warahram (victory), Ram (breath of life) and
Wad (divinity of wind and space), and the rest of the days are dedicated to the
following: Daena (revelation), Ard (reward), Arshtad (honesty), Asman (sky),
Zam/Zamyad (earth), Maraspand or Manthra Spenta (sacred invocation), An-
eran/Anaghra Raocha (endless light). Alongside its meaningful name, each
day has a flower (fragrant plant) dedicated to it. However, the idea is not to
make the scent of flowers into a sign of divinity: the naming of the days in the
Zoroastrian calendar has cultural rather than religious significance.

The Zoroastrian calendar makes connections between the scent of flowers
and plants, on the one hand, and the passage of time, on the other, so that
olfaction is made to signify spatial and temporal awareness in addition to its
aesthetic significance. The types of flowers representing each day indicate
the place and the season in which they grow. 'Banug-spraham' is the flower
attached to the 'goddess of earth' in the day-naming. This flower blossoms in
late winter and early spring and the last month of winter is called 'Spandar-
Maz' or 'goddess of earth'.

The emphasis in this system of day-naming through flowers is specifically
on odour and not (for example) their visual beauty or their ephemeral nature
compared to other plants. The system resonates with the field of subjectivity,
and this resonance will be elaborated in more detail in the chapter on the olfactory drive. In such an approach, smell becomes a means to index the Real
register of our being based on our temporal orientation.

The philosophy behind such a correlation between fragrant flowers and the
name of the days differs from the Hebrew and Christian belief in the sweet
smell of sanctity. The duality of the stench of hell, sin and evil, on one hand,
and the sweet smell of heaven, martyrdom, holiness, salvation and sanctity,
on the other, has been much used in theological, cosmological and mythical
literatures since Antiquity. The duality follows the basic principle of the pleasant and unpleasant. Odours in this approach belong to the field of Other: we
have a dynamic between the subject and his or her construction of the Other
or, in this context, God or gods. When smell becomes a sign of divinity, its status changes to an indicator of presence and communication, as can be shown
by referring to some historical accounts of the senses and divinity and to the
traditional association between smelling, seeing and hearing and the perception of divinity. Smelling, of all the senses, is most involved in 'invoking' and
'evoking' a holy presence. (Clements, 2014). In various religious practices,
the offering of sweet, pleasant fragrances to the gods was a way of attracting
their favourable attention. In Roman religion, smell was an integral part of
the sacrificial rituals, carried out for the satisfaction of the gods, as well as an
indication of their presence, and this thinking has clear avatars in Christian
olfactory culture (Toner, 2014).

Lionel Rothkrug in an article on 'The "Odour of Sanctity," and the Hebrew Origins of Christian Relic Veneration' notes that it was a common belief in late Antiquity and the early Middle Ages that most Christian saints received their sainthood after death, and the first and significant sign of their holiness was a pleasant odour or 'sweet smell' emitted from their bones when their bodies were exhumed. The agreeable smell (absence of the smell of decay) in the tomb was evidence of their eternal life after death, unaffected by the sinful, desiring body. The biblical literature of both Judaism and Christianity highlights the role of pleasant odours in ceremonial rituals, as a sign of God's approval or His willingness to accept atonement (Rothkrug, 1981).

Situating odours in the field of the Other has another theoretical consequence for olfactory experience. It makes the sense of smell into a moral sense, particularly as to the question of enjoyment. In many religious practices, the sense of smell is subject to suppression and renunciation whenever scents are associated with sexual attraction, pleasure or sensuality. The paradoxical effect at the level of language is that the most pleasing aroma is transformed into the stench of sin.

The nose as the organ of smell has received philosophical and metaphorical treatment in language. In medieval texts, smell and the nose were signs of power and social status as well as of sexuality and temptation. Mutilation of the nose, as the most visible organ on the face, was an accepted form of punishment for sexual promiscuity and other crimes during the medieval period and, in earlier times, for treachery. Mark Bradley and Eric Varner in an article, 'Missing Noses', argue that the intention of such a brutal punishment was to deprive miscreants of olfactory experience and to make breathing difficult for them. (Bradley & Varner, 2014). As shown by more recent anatomical findings, these effects were not in fact obtained since the centre of sense perception analysis and breathing is in the brain and not in the nose. But the intention of depriving the person of enjoyment in life (smelling and comfortable breathing) was clear, alongside the visible warning to others in the community of the punishment that could be expected for certain crimes.

Marcel Proust's treatment in *Swann's Way* (the first part of *In Search of Lost Time*) of the connection between the senses of smell and taste and remembering the past is justifiably famous. The writer describes how 'involuntary memory' arises when taking a bite from a madeleine cake (Proust, 1981). The taste and smell of the delicacy bring long-dormant memories from childhood flooding back to consciousness: the experience of Sunday mornings at his aunt's house where he was given a madeleine to eat after his aunt had first soaked it in her own cup of lime-blossom cordial. The taste of the madeleine takes the narrator back to the town and home of his childhood. Proust shows how a journey into the past, starting from an involuntary memory, turns into an active/voluntary search for times past, conjuring up an elaborate picture of the surroundings and experience of familiar spaces from the past. His descriptive language, based on olfactory experience, succeeds in expressing a sense of enjoyment, as if the narrator takes pleasure in the very act of going back to, searching for and eventually reviving what was lost. From the immediacy of involuntary memory, 'catapulted' to the subject, to the lingering effect of an olfactory experience, we have an active search for the essence of the past. We can ask here: what is this essence of the past that has been given such ample space by the subject? From the psychoanalytic point of view, what is lost needs to remain lost (like the myth of Eden) as a precondition for the formation of a desire, which can move or circulate around that lost object. Olfactory experience facilitates this process.

I began this chapter with a poem by Baudelaire about the aroma from an antique phial that transports the sniffer to another dimension of time. Odours have the power of infiltrating forgotten memories, allowing a subject to re-live a past experience, but they can also block out unwanted memories, and intoxication with a scent can cause a desirable oblivion. In another poem, *Lethe*, Baudelaire writes of seeking oblivion away from a cruel reality in the intoxicating smell, touch and kisses of his lover where Lethe (the underworld river of oblivion) flows:

'To bury my head, full of pain
In your skirt redolent of your perfume,
To inhale, as from a withered flower,
The moldy sweetness of my defunct love.'
        (Baudelaire, 2015, p. 215)

As can be seen, our olfactory experience is highly influenced by culture and language. Despite the visualist culture, which has come to the fore in the recent history of our civilisation, and regardless of the requisitioning of the sense of smell by cultural studies, it is as a subject of the unconscious, whose being is subject to the acquisition of language, that we most need our sense of smell. Olfaction is a culture-born experience as well as a sensory faculty and if it is lost in one, it can appear in the other. When a patient of mine had lost her sense of smell during the recent pandemic, she developed an involuntary experience of the smell of favourite meals from her childhood. Even if we label such an experience as an olfactory hallucination, we still need to ask why she experienced that particular smell? Why is there a need to be reminded of childhood not through the olfactory sense itself, but through an olfactory memory? Detailed accounts of olfactory experience or references to smelling in literature are perhaps an attempt to drag a bodily excitation into words not only in order to preserve it, but also in the hope that the reader can share the experience. Literary descriptions in terms of vision and sound may fail to make a fantasy as 'real' as possible or to convey an intense, immediate transportation into a fantastical or real scene, and the element of mystery in any story is almost always associated with a non-visual experience (the invisible).

Smell and also the voice, as invisible objects of the olfactory and invocatory faculties, are paramount in interpreting our experience of a mysterious presence. Visuality, which is equated with revelation, unmasking or appearance/reappearance, works in opposition to mystery. Seeing strange things is not the same as perplexity or anxiety concerning a mysterious encounter at the level of our sense perception. In biblical accounts, the impossibility of seeing God and remaining alive is another way of understanding how the scopic faculty is redundant compared with smelling or hearing when it comes to perception beyond the reality principle. As discussed above, descriptions in literature of invoking or communicating with gods refer to the olfactory and auditory faculties. The responses of our scopic faculty in relation to mysterious or uncanny experience – the avoidance of seeing or, conversely, our emphasis on seeing the object that causes anxiety – show how our visuality attempts to symbolise and index a real experience. In producing a tangible knowledge and form of enjoyment for the subject, scopic information indexes the mystery, rather than offering or allowing the subject to enjoy the mystery beyond the Symbolic.

A smell artist, Anicka Yi, believes that people tend to associate invisibility and smell with the feminine, while visuality and knowledge are usually associated with the masculine (Jeffreis, 2021).

Such a division may be problematic as a phenomenological distinction between smell and sight at the level of the individual, and we may disagree from a psychoanalytical perspective with such gendering of mystery and knowledge, but Yi's statement is nonetheless thought-provoking. Unlike sight, smell mystifies and penetrates invisibility rather than indexing it. As discussed earlier in this chapter, philosophy has tended to give primacy to sight among the other senses based on the range of information, which this sense can provided to us. The feminine-masculine distinction in relation to knowledge and to smell and sight can be linked with the Lacanian treatment of sexuality. If we take the masculine and feminine as two different positions in relation to phallic and beyond-phallic (Other) jouissance, sight, as a knowledge-providing sense, has a close affinity with phallic jouissance, which always fails to fully satisfy the subject, while smell aligns with the Other jouissance, which exceeds and goes beyond any symbolisation. At the level of gender identity, access to each form of enjoyment is quite possible for both a man and a woman. Coprophilic or perfume fetishists occur in any sexual orientation. Indeed, from this perspective, the sense of smell can be formulated as a lost sense in two sets of theories on feminine sexuality. Firstly, when sexuality is formulated as an access to phallic or Other jouissance and the sense of smell correlates with the latter as specifically feminine. Secondly, when scent is used as a type of masquerade. The latter is an attempt to either hide or represent a social status. In the psychoanalytic literature, masquerade is associated with feminine sexuality and it is understood as one possible, symbolic way of accessing womanhood.

How can our sense perceptions be understood and perhaps formulated through the psychoanalytic lens? What sort of consequences do our senses and specifically olfaction have on our subjectivity? We can elaborate these questions further by looking at the psychoanalytic literature.

The Psychoanalytic Nose

Olfaction was an important question for Freud. It is worth investigating how the father of psychoanalysis approached the sense of smell – as a lost sense or, conversely, as a sense that is at the heart of his theory of repression and the origin of neurosis.

As discussed in the previous chapter, 'What is Smell?', Freud's treatment of the sense of smell starts by exploring the question of enjoyment and the abandonment of olfactory satisfaction together with that derived from excitation of the mouth, throat, nose and anus. Freud equates what he calls 'organic repression' with renunciation of satisfaction from stimulation of these libidinal zones. He conjectures that the adoption by the human race of an upright, two-legged posture reflects this abandonment of olfactory satisfaction. However, by referring to such a loss of olfactory satisfaction (organic repression) during evolution, Freud is not downplaying the importance of olfaction. He is, rather, giving a formative role to the loss, which eventually leads humans to find a way to deal with the organic repression while surviving and acquiring language as civilised beings. His theory of both repression and human sexuality begins with a clear reference to the loss of olfactory satisfaction. So, the question of satisfaction is highlighted. From this perspective, we can say that smell has a formative role in our subjectivity and in the constitution of psychoanalysis. In a letter to his friend Wilhelm Fliess dated 14th November 1897, Freud writes:

> ... I have often suspected that something organic played a part in repression; I was able once before to tell you that it was a question of the abandonment of former sexual zones ... the notion was linked to the changed part played by sensations of smell: upright carriage adopted, nose raised from the ground, at the same time a number of formerly interesting sensations attached to the earth becoming repulsive.
>
> (Freud, 1897, p. 268)

Earlier in the same year, in a letter of 11th January 1897, Freud compared the status of the sense of smell in humans with its status as the 'principle' sense in other animals, stressing that the sense of smell in humans did not serve the same survival purposes that it serves for animals – in their sexual, hunting, eating, etc., behaviours. But although olfaction has lost those 'animalistic' functionalities in humans, it has remained sexually exciting for us. He concludes that the smell of the body, hair, faeces and blood can have arousal effects. So, olfaction, in Freud's view, remains a vibrant sense through its contribution to sexual enjoyment. He connects the privileged role of the sense of smell in some people with the emotion of disgust (more in girls than boys, as he asserts). Disgust as an affect in Freud's early definition of hysteria and so-called 'hysterical anaesthesia' were both related to the sense of smell. (Freud, 1897, p. 241)

As can be seen, Freud emphasised the sense of smell among all other functions, which were blunted or even lost by humans in the process of the civilisation. But while acknowledging that olfaction is no longer of importance for survival, he gives it new status as playing a pivotal role in repression and the genesis of neurosis, where two questions are always in play – the questions of sexuality and enjoyment.

Some commentators have speculated that Freud's attention to the sense of smell was a result of his friendship with Fliess, who was an ear, nose and throat specialist and who developed and put forward his 'nasal reflex neurosis' theory in the 1890s. Fliess believed in a relationship between the genitals and the nose, which caused patients to suffer from neuro-psychological conditions, which could be cured by surgical intervention. Fliess's theory compared the smell organ with the sex organ on the basis of certain physiological changes during menstruation and pregnancy. This odd equation led him to the idea of treating dysmenorrhea and painful labour by surgical and cocaine interventions on the nose. Freud famously linked the 'hysteria' of his patient Emma Eckstein's with her excessive masturbation and offered her a cauterising nasal cavity operation performed by Fliess. The intervention proved disastrous. Fliess mistakenly left a 50-centimetre piece of surgical gauze in the patient's nose and she remained disfigured for the rest of her life. Freud's dream of Irma's injection, which has been interpreted as expressing Freud's guilt at encouraging Eckstein to undergo surgery, is of crucial importance for the invention of psychoanalysis.

This early attention to odours in Freud's work of the 1890s foreshadows his later elaborations concerning sexual perversions such as fetishism and coprophilia. According to Freud, the upright posture of humans, the shift of emphasis from the sense of smell to that of sight and the associated emergence of cleanness as a human imperative, led to the first organic repression – olfactive repression, which was instrumental in the genesis of disgust and the loss of pleasure in the smell of excrement and genitals. However, the clinic of psychoanalysis, past and present, testifies that smells, culturally pleasant in the form of perfume or unpleasant as the odour of excrement and the genitals, are essential ingredients of sexual fantasy and sexual practices.

Whether or not we agree with Freud's thesis on the relationship between the formation of neurosis and olfactory repression due to evolution and civilisation, the sense of smell has certainly never been a lost sense. Freud labelled it an 'original pleasure' the presence of which continues to influence our social and sexual being. Discussing fetishism in a letter to Karl Abraham of 24th February 1910, Freud says that the smell of the fetish object matters more than its visual image or its feel. He describes the case of a 25-year-old man, a clothing and shoe fetishist and a voyeur since his teenage years, obsessed with his appearance and dress, and with a history of coprophilia between the ages of eight and ten. The young man was a 'over-sensitive smeller' and had even kept a hard sausage in his rectum for a period in his childhood, eating small pieces from it through the day. Freud concludes as follows:

> I have learnt from other cases that shoe fetishism goes back to an original pleasure (olfactory pleasure) in the dirty and stinking foot. This indeed recurs in the positive perversion. I regard coprophilic olfactory pleasure as being the chief factor in most cases of foot and shoe fetishism.
>
> (Abraham, 2002, P. 106)

A year earlier, in February 1909, Freud had written to Abraham that in foot fetishism, the olfactory pleasure is 'driven out' and the original object (the foul-smelling foot) is elevated to a fetish object. The same mechanism was to be found when the fetish was women's clothing. Freud elaborates the pleasure of a passive scopic drive (to be seen), as in exhibitionism, as the replacement of an original pleasure obtained from the olfactory drive. This will be discussed in more detail in the chapter dedicated to the concept of drive and olfaction.

Privilege given to the smell of sweaty clothes or underwear is not uncommon in experience of the clinic of perversion. In such cases, the smell itself, rather than a particular piece of clothing, is the fetish object (olfactory fetishism). Similarly, sniffers take olfactory pleasure in the odour emitted by fragrant objects and perfumes (perfume sniffers are less likely than underwear sniffers to seek psychoanalytic treatment and it is interesting that extreme fondness for perfumes and perfumery is considered to be a sublimation, while coprophilia and urophilia are treated as perverse sexual acts). As was already discussed, olfactory pleasure, like other sensual pleasures (scopic, invocatory, tactile and taste), is socially and individually influenced by culture. So, the socio-cultural aspect of olfaction can play an important role in whether or not a person seeks treatment for an olfactory mode of enjoyment. In the clinic, the subject's olfaction-related complaints can indicate different underlying stances towards olfactory experience. In one case of severe olfactory obsession, it was not only bad smells that were not tolerated – the natural odour of the skin was also found offensive. Covering the body with perfume was a way of avoiding an overpowering disgust towards the natural fragrance of the subject's own body and the bodies of other people. In this case, the smell of perfume was a defence against disgust rather than an object of enjoyment.

What can the scent of our own body mean for our subjectivity from a psychoanalytic viewpoint? Where can it be located in our being? We might start with the distinction between presence and absence. Odour is a particularly powerful symbol of someone's presence. During the Covid-19 pandemic, when meetings in person were prohibited and most social interactions, including psychoanalysis, were conducted remotely (online or by phone), touch and smell were markedly absent from our interchange with others. Also, anosmia (temporary loss of the sense of smell) due to infection by the virus caused extreme mental anguish in some subjects specifically because they were unable to smell their own bodies. The sense of alienation from one's own self went so far in some cases that the body was perceived as a dead mass. In another clinical case, the subject's anxiety was focused on her inability to experience the smell of her young children. For her, smell and smelling were closely tied up with her feminine position and with maternity. Olfaction facilitated her access to her femininity as a subject in the Symbolic order and her language was filled with references to olfaction, from the use of scents of natural origin in her living space to the use of perfume on her body. During the period of prolonged lockdown, when analysis in person was not possible, she complained of missing the smell of the consulting room. During her anosmia, her main concern was not losing a source of pleasure, but of losing her sense of being. In this and similar cases odours were not merely exotic stimulants, eliciting a particular form of joy – the ability to sense smells had become a powerful compass for existing as a speaking being. So, smell can be a marker of our being and it can also signify our mortality, but not in the simplistic sense of an association between bad odour and putrefaction (as discussed in the health and care professions), but because our being is born into a smelly environment, from the womb onwards, that lack of smell becomes a sign of death and life in a scent-free environment is unbearable. The de-odorisation of urban spaces followed by their re-odorisation with pleasant artificial smells is thought-provoking in this respect.

In discussions of invocation as it pertains to the theory of the drive, Lacanian literature has mainly focused on hearing. But, as discussed earlier, in the history of religions, the gods or God have also been invoked through smell, when believers offer their sacrifices through fire, incense or perfume. It is, of course, not surprising that Lacanians associate invocation with sound and not smell, since listening to narratives is the main analytic act and that which marks psychoanalysis as a talking cure. The act of listening to the sound and the equivocal meaning of words, to the said or to the unspoken, to the sound of a subject's silence, to the narrative of the body and beyond, is what is generally considered as the constitutive factor of psychoanalysis. However, in the consulting room, on occasions where smell becomes a signifier or takes the status of a symptom, invoking (or not invoking) a response (interpretation) from the Other, a sensory object becomes a narrative – a 'smelly narrative'!

One case in point is that of a male analysand whose own smelly body functioned as a medium, by which he gauged his place in the Other's desire. He omitted to take regular showers and maintain personal hygiene, initially blaming it on lack of time. Deeper reasons for this attitude emerged as the analysis progressed and he came back to the odour of his body in the context of a complaint he had heard from an ex-girlfriend: he suggested that he failed to wash on purpose, in order to test how much his lover desired him. He suffered from an inability to make major decisions in life and had a difficult love life. The issue that brought him to analysis was a numbness in his feet, which he had instantly interpreted as an incurable paralysis, although a medical examination found no real condition that could explain the sensation. Immobility, literal and metaphorical, was, in fact, dominant in the picture that he described of himself. He was almost always late for his sessions, had a habit of spending hours in the toilet due to long-term and persistent constipation, was sleepy in sessions and at work, and avoided socialising with colleagues and peers. After detailed exploration of his past and childhood, he settled on two signifiers: his mother, whom he often referred to as a distant and cold caregiver towards her children, had described him as 'smelly' and 'sleepy' boy since birth. Surprisingly, he found nothing offensive in either of the words. Why he had identified with those traits and how had he interpreted such a narrative for the meaning of his being for the Other (signification), became the focus of our analysis at that stage of the work. Later, he also admitted that he enjoyed the smell of his own faeces as well as seeing expressions of disgust in the face or body language of other people. At the level of his mode of enjoyment, he was an 'odour exhibitionist' and having a foul smell was his symptom. His avoidance of social interactions indicated a contradictory position towards his smell. He purposely became smelly (showering only once a week) before going out with friends and colleagues, and then felt anxious while in their company in case his smell might disgust them. So, the interpretation of a narrative of the first caregiver had formed the core of his symptom. This invocation, originating from the field of the Other contained a clear reference to the smell of the body. Later, the subject's construction of this reference functioned as an invocation to the Other's desire, while also offering an enjoyment to the subject at the level of drive.

The reading of the above case, in respect of symptom formation, the Other's desire and drive montage, hinged on an early narrative with a sensual and bodily reference. So, smell in this case, as in many others, was an ever-present sense and not a lost sense. At the level of subject formation, of the first identification and of alienation from the m(O)ther, the sense of smell precedes hearing from a psychoanalytic perspective. This point will be elaborated in more detail in the rest of this chapter. In the chapter on the olfactory drive, we will expand on the role of smell as a bodily presence in the formation of the drive montage.

Communication

At the level of intersubjective relations, odours are famous and notorious for breaking through the wall of language and creating their own narrative. Smell does not recognise the borders and boundaries of the Other of language.

On the other hand, it is an indicator of recognition of others, of spaces and of times. Françoise Dolto emphasises that smell is the first sense used by the subject to recognise his or her principle caregiver – the bodily Other, distinct from the subject's own body, is recognised through the mediation of smell and voice before the infant's vision is properly developed. In particular, smell signals proximity of the Other and Dolto concludes that juxtaposition of voice and smell creates a sense of space for the child (a way of gauging distance from the Other).

Smell is the strongest signal of the mother's presence, enabling the child to experience a dimension beyond its own body, the first recognition laying the foundation for subsequent alienation and separation. Dolto examines olfaction at the level of separation anxiety, transmission of affects and the mother-child communication. We will discuss the relationship between smell and separation during infancy and childhood (at the level of subject formation) in more depth in the chapter 'What is smell?' For Dolto, there is an olfactive language of affects, which is transmissible between two subjects (specifically in the mOther-child bond) – the smell of fear, agitation, joy, sadness, anger, rage, etc. Is that not another way of saying that the language of odours precedes the language of spoken words, punctuating the mother-child communication?

We will examine some clinical aspects of a similar case in the next part, where olfaction plays a fundamental role in mother and child bounding, subjective interpretation of a silent narrative and the significance of smell and smelling at the level of the drive arrangement.

In the formation of the subject in the register of language, where the organic body is marked by language, coming-into-being begins with separation from the Other. According to Lacan, the first introduction to the symbolic order happens for a subject in the mirror stage, when he or she encounters their image in the mirror. The child is never alone with their image: a third party either does or does not facilitate the child's introduction to the world of signifiers (the Symbolic) based on the description of the image. But one important aspect of interaction with the external world, before the mirror experience, is missed here – namely the register of olfaction. In babies, the sense of smell is more developed than the sense of vision (the organic development of both hearing and touch advance more quickly than that of vision). Smell, even more than touch, can be considered the most immediate and 'closest' sense employed by the new-born subject to connect with the caregiver, either for establishing a bond or for meeting its vital needs. The smell of the mother's body when she is fearful, or when she is agitated or anxious, as well as the smell of the mother's milk in such situations can cause the baby to refuse comfort or refuse to eat.

Another clinical example will help to illustrate this. The mother of a six-month-old baby girl was referred to talking therapy after seeing a paediatrician due to concerns about her child, who was holding its breath. The mother's narrative produced more details of the trigger and the context in which such episodes were taking place. Both the mother and the paediatrician concluded that the behaviour was the child's protest against separation from the mother. However, it emerged that the child also held its breath when such separation was not a threat and it became clear in the therapy that issues on the side of the mother herself were a contributing factor. She was already a mother of two children and had a difficult relationship with her partner. She had become pregnant with the latest child after finding out that her partner was having an affair and after they had decided for that reason not to have any more children. The mother was an introverted woman, brought up to not to complain about her difficulties. Her body, however, was unable to conceal the truth of her suffering and when she experienced either rage or anxiety, she came out in a sweat that produced an acidic odour. This odour emerged in her narrative when she was recounting her partner's complaints against her in the relationship. She admitted that she had frequently experienced such distressing moments while holding or breast-feeding her baby girl and that the child had then stopped sucking her nipple and begun an episode of breath holding.

We may ask: why did the child choose this particular way of refusing milk instead of (for example) throwing a tantrum to express anger, frustration or fright? At the level of language, 'withholding' complaints and 'breathing no words' are evidently present on the side of the mother. On that basis some Lacanians may emphasise the invisible effect of the narrative of the mother – her silence in response to hardship – on the child's way of exercising its agency. But a different narrative of the Real body, which was sweating with rage and fear, emitting an acidic smell of fear, is surely also at stake here. Could it not be that this bodily narrative – the language of smell – was sufficient to give the child an immediate, intuitive reading of the situation? It is certainly true that, at the organic level, hormonal imbalances affect the taste and smell of a mother's milk.

Conclusion

Is smell really a lost sense? Olfaction plays a fundamental role as a marker of home, of belonging, anchoring one's being through an interplay between the subject and the Other. Smelling the space where we feel safe, repeating the same food, experiencing the passage of seasons/time, intimacy, deodorising and re-odorising our bodies and surroundings, breathing life and feeling alive, avoiding certain odours, diving into the intensity of pleasure offered by a perfume or even by a stench – for some of us smell is life. Losing the ability to smell one's own body can be deeply destabilising for some people.

I have attempted to approach the rhetorical question in the title of this chapter by exploring different dimensions of sense perception, both at the level of the body and of language, from an analytic perspective. The aim, using examples from the clinic of psychoanalysis, works of literature and the medical understanding of olfaction, was to ask why the sense of smell is not considered or theorised in the analytic literature to the same extent as the other senses. The use of 'lost' to describe the olfactory sense is meant to connote the idea of a 'lost paradise' as understood in psychoanalysis, which views nostalgia for something lost as an essential ingredient when a begins their journey in life. In Lacanian psychoanalysis, the object causes of desire (the 'object little a') is a remainder of an enjoyment at the level of the body, which has been cut off by language. This lost object is a remainder, an excess or a forbidden jouissance, which is at the same time a precondition for the formation of the subject of the unconscious. This lost object is what moves the subject's desire, and the drives circulate around it. As I have tried to show in this chapter, the ever-present olfactory sense both forms and punctuates our mode of being. Smell is essential for the formation of the subject and has an immortal and continuous presence in our lives.

The next chapter will ask whether the role of olfaction, as a lost and yet present sense, is limited to the concept of the drive.

Bibliography

Abraham, K. (2002). *The Complete Correspondences of Sigmund Freud & Karl Abraham 1907–1925*. London: Routledge

Atchley, E. (2015). *A History of the Use of Incense in Divine Worship*, 1909. Andesite Press

Azarnouche, S. (2013). *Husraw I Kawadan Ud Redag-E (Khosrow Fils Du Kawad Et Un Page)* Edit & Trans. Leuven: Peeters Press

Bahar, M. (2009). *Bundahish, Franbagh Dadagi (Edition)*. Tehran: Toos Publication

Baudelaire, C. (2015). *The Flowers of the Evil, Les Fleurs Du Mal, English and French Edition*, William Ageller (Trans). Digireads Publishing

Baltussen, H. (2014). Ancient Philosophers on the Sense of Smell. pp. 30–46. In: *Smell and the Ancient Senses, by Bradley*, M. London: Routledge

Bradley, M. & Varner, E. (2014). Missing Noses pp. 171–181. In: *Smell and the Ancient Senses*, by Bradley, M. London: Routledge

Classon, C. (1994). The Aromas of Antiquity. pp. 13–25. In: *Aroma: The Cultural History of Smell*, (eds). London: Routledge

Clements, A. (2014). Divine Scents and Presence. pp. 46–60. In: *Smell and the Ancient Senses, by Bradley*, M. London: Routledge

Elgood, C. (2010). *A Medical History of Persia and the Eastern Caliphate: From the Earliest Times Until the Year A.D. 1932* Cambridge: Cambridge University Press

Epictetus (2022). *Epictetus The Complete Works Handbook: Discourses and Fragments*, Robin Waterfield (TRANS): Chicago: The University of Chicago Press

Freud, S. (1897). Letter 75. Pre-Psycho-Analytic Publications and Unpublished Drafts (1886–1889). pp. 268–272. In: J. *Strachey, ed. The Standard Edition of the Complete Psychological Works of Sigmund Freud, Vol. I*. London: Vintage, 2001

Gignoux, P. (2001). *Man & Cosmos in Ancient Iran*. Rome: Is. I.A.O

Horne, C. F. (2010). *The Vendidad: The Zoroastrian Book of The Law*. Kessinger Pub Lic

Jeffries, S. (2021). The Guardians Interview: https://www.theguardian.com/artanddesign/2021/oct/06/anicka-yi-tate-modern-turbine-hall-commission?CMP=share_btn_wa

Lacan, J. (1953–4). *The Seminar of Jacques Lacan: Book 1: Freud's Papers on Technique.* John Forrester (Trans). The United States: Norton

Lacan, J. (1963–4). *The Seminar of Jacque Lacan: Book XI: Four Fundamental Concepts of Psychoanalysis.* Alan Sheridan (Trans). New York & London: Norton

Le Guerer, A. (1992). *Scent: The Mysterious and Essential Powers of Smell.* Miller, R. (Trans). New York: Turtle Bay Books

Mackenzie, D. N. (1971). *A Concise Pahlavi Dictionary.* London: Routledge

Proust, M. (1981). *In Search of the Lost Time: Vol.1 Swann's Way.* London: Everyman Publishers plc

Rothkrug, L. (1981). 'The "Odour of Sanctity," and the Hebrew Origins of Christian Relic Veneration. pp. 95–95. In: *Historical Reflections.* Vol. 8, No. 2. Oxford: Berghhan Books

Toner, J. (2014). Smell and Christianity, pp. 158–171. In: *Smell and the Ancient Senses, by Bradley, M.* London: Routledge

Wahman, F. (2018). *Ardā Wirāz Nāmag: The Iranian 'Divina Commedia'.* London: Routledge

Chapter 4

Is There an Olfactory Drive?

Introduction

The drive is an essential psychoanalytical concept with a primitive and sexual nature, which has a common root with the formation of our psychical life. The drive lies at the heart of human sexuality and makes the difference between human sexuality and that of other animals. Unlike the sexual life of other animals, the drive in the sexuality of the human subject emerges with the unconscious, acting as a force that moves the subject towards the other outside the self. The drive function is not simply an act of self-preservation, as are the instincts in the animal, but is an excitation that gives a sense of liveliness to the living body of the subject. In Freud's work drive, function is exemplified by the partial sexual drives. The body, which is not perceived merely as an organic being, is both the origin and the destination of the drive. The four characteristics of each drive are pressure, aim, source and object. Beginning with internal pressure, the drive, unlike need, which aims at immediate and full satisfaction, has many ways of dealing with the question of satisfaction. The object of the drive, as an external or internal object at the level of the body, is not an actual and fixed object, but is rather a lost object and is described as such in the analytical literature. The lost object defines the aim of the drive as a search for something, which promises complete satisfaction but remains elusive and indefinable. It is precisely the absence of the object that introduces the symbolic dimension to the subject. The emergence of the drive is bound up with the symbolic order. From the first cry of the new-born child, the drive is shaped in the Other's presence. So, the psychical life of the subject comes into being with the drive and this cannot happen without the Other. Finally, the source of the drive is somewhere between body and psyche, or the subject's Real body in a Lacanian sense. This gives rise to another dimension of our being: the Real.

The focus of this chapter will be olfaction as it relates to the concept of the drive. Can we consider the faculty of smell as a distinct montage of the drive-in human sexuality?

The first component of the olfactory drive is pressure, which assumes a rhythmic quality (as does any other form of the drive for a baby in the physical

DOI: 10.4324/9781003485322-4

absence/presence of the caregiver, milk and bodily wastes). The aim of the olfactory drive can be understood as seeking a satisfaction/dissatisfaction in the form of reassurance when being held, fed or encouraged to sleep (smell as a complementary companion to other modes of oral or tactile satisfaction), or when soiling or being cleaned (smell as an indicator of cleanness/dirtiness that comes before tactile or anal satisfaction).

Smell, as the object of the olfactory drive, has been little studied in the psychoanalytical literature, a neglect which parallels the lack of attention to olfaction compared with the other senses in philosophical treatments of human perception. We can venture some hypotheses as to why odour was not given a place among other libidinal objects (faeces, gaze, voice and later the skin) in both the Freudian and Lacanian traditions. We might think, for example, that smell has not been much studied in the history of psychoanalysis to date because the presence of smell at the level of the mother-child relationship was taken for granted. It is worth briefly exploring various dimensions of such presence. Smell, having the most primitive nature as compared with the other types of the drive, marks the formation of the subject of the unconscious by punctuating and conditioning the subject's relation to their first significant Other, on whom they are dependent at the level of demand. The smell of the caregiver's body during the activities of being fed, caressed, getting changed and prepared for sleep is essential company for a baby. So, smelling finds an economy of demand, which is incapable of complete satisfaction and is expressed in order to be frustrated. The fragrances of the mother's garment or skin, which have a unique character for each baby, are looked for, recognised and demanded over and over, every time a child is held. The odour of the child's own body or bodily wastes (faeces, urine and breath) can also signify how much they are cared (loved) for by the Other. Moreover, experiencing hunger, thirst, cleanness or dirtiness generates uncomfortable sensations at the level of the subject's stomach or skin, while generating a distinct odour, and the objects of the oral and anal drives (breast, faeces) have a particular smell/odour. But that is not to suggest that smell is merely a complementary/companion object to the other drive objects. The smell of mother can be fantasised and looked for as much as nourishment, visual image and voice or tactile qualities such as softness, warmth, being held or being caressed.

The source of the olfactory drive libidinises the subject's body through the way in which a mother cares for her child. All the chores of care, from feeding to changing nappies or smelling one's child in order to check its state of health or show affection will mark the Real body at the level of sexuality. If a child is in the care of too many different people or if its body is treated as a locus/instrument for an operational function, the source of the drive is disturbed and the circulation of the drive around the object is obstructed. Later in this chapter, I will refer to some clinical cases in order to expand on disruptions of olfactory drive characteristics, which can result in symptom formation in childhood or in adult life.

The subject's relation to the sense of smell is present from birth to such a degree that one cannot imagine the formation of the subject without a significant role for olfaction. As discussed earlier in this book, olfaction, as an intuitive sense, enters the domain of language as much as the tactile, auditory and visual senses, and can be employed to address a subjective interpretation of knowledge and truth. At the level of language, 'smelling a truth' or 'smelling a reality' is just as valid as observing/witnessing, hearing an echo of, or being in touch with/perceiving the touch of a subjective reality. The sensory references in a subject's narrative can also point to an unconscious phantasy as a scenario of his or her symptom, which has its roots in the drive. In other words, the arrangement of a specific drive is manifest in language and language has a constitutive role in it. Moreover, verbal references can say something about the focus of the libido in the psychical life of a subject. For instance, it makes sense to describe a person's character as more or less visual, tactile, oral, anal, auditory or olfactive, and this usually indicates how much a subject has invested libidinally in a specific sensory faculty. This does not only reflect a quality of the subject's character but can also signify a mode of enjoyment, which is gained through a specific drive for a subject at the level of his or her body and psyche. Olfaction, among all of the senses, is that which is the most intimate and closest to the subject's experience of intuitive knowledge. One possible reason for the importance of olfaction in language and its specifically intuitive nature is that smelling happens through breathing. Our life is dependent on breathing in a way that is much more immediate than, for example, our dependence on nourishment or warmth. The olfactory faculty is intertwined with the act of breathing. It circulates inside and outside the body through respiration.

The linkage between olfaction and respiration is indeed crucial and will receive closer attention in a separate chapter later in this book. For now, we will stay focused on the origin and destiny of olfaction in relation to the concept of the drive-in psychoanalysis. The next step, therefore, is to examine Freudian and Lacanian readings of the drive and link them to the developing discussion of the olfactory drive.

Re-reading the Freudian Invention: The Drive

The Imaginary dimension of the drive-in clinical material can be observed at the level of the subject's narratives on his/her sex or romantic life or it can be expressed in the Real of the neurotic's symptom, since symptom formation has its roots in the concept of the drive. As I will go on to discuss in detail, Freud situates the drive at the heart of human sexuality at least since his *Three Essays on the Theory of Sexuality* (Freud, 1905). He used the concept in order to draw a clear distinction between human sexuality and the rhythmic and cyclical mating and reproduction behaviour of other animals. Freud sees the drives as partial and unruly prior to puberty, as expressed in the 'polymorphous perversity' of children. After puberty, the drives become focused on a so-called 'erogenous zone'. Constantly seeking pleasure (the pleasure principle), the drive has no specific object and is not directed towards an aim for the purpose of gaining absolute satisfaction.

Olfaction had an early presence in Freud's thinking when he was elaborating the relation between so-called 'organic repression' and our subjectivity. Our main aim here is not to respond to the question, why olfaction has not been given more space in the analytic literature, but to explore whether or not olfaction can find a place in the Freudian invention that he called 'the drive'. If our approach to olfaction is to reduce it to the drive, what consequences does such an approach have for us in the clinic of psychoanalysis?

I will try to take up a critical stance towards any reductive approach to the theory and clinic of psychoanalysis. To do so, I will start with the trajectory of the concept of the drive in Freud's work before turning to Lacan's contribution to this rather ambiguous; yet, fundamental Freudian concept, in order to understand how an olfactory drive can play a role in or contribute to our subjectivity or our 'knot of being' in the Lacanian sense. Many analysts, including Lacan himself, consider the concept of the drive to be as fundamental and important as the concept of the unconscious and label it as Freud's most original invention.

Freud's concept of *Trieb* (drive) dates back to 1895, when he wrote the *Project for a Scientific Psychology*. He starts with a child's physiological needs (hunger/thirst) and the question of satisfaction. An urge within the child calls upon the other to provide a satisfactory response to such 'endogenous stimuli', which are continuously present but which become psychical stimuli in periodic fashion (Freud, 1895, p. 316). The feelings of 'urgency' and 'effort to discharge' are released, producing 'expression of emotions and screaming' (Freud, 1895, p. 317) or a cry for help on the part of the infant. This discharge of an 'internal change'/impulse has as its result the provision of attention and care by the Other. In this way, the discharge acquires a 'secondary function' – that of communication with the Other, to which Freud attached greater importance than the mere satisfaction of a physiological need. Moreover, Freud makes the human subject's helplessness in relation to such stimuli/impulses and their inevitable discharge through crying and screaming into 'the primal source of all moral motives'. (Freud, 1895, p. 318) To Freud, at this early stage of his work, the image of the caregiver who satisfies the infant's need at the time of wishing/urgency – the 'memory of the object' – can be hallucinated. As is evident from many mother-and-child clinical cases in the history of psychoanalysis and from the everyday experience of mothers with their babies, the remembered object does not have to be the image of the care giver. The smell of the mother's garment or body can function as the memory of the object, which, according to Freud, is hallucinated when the state of urgency (need) recurs. Freud says that this 'wishful activation' (hallucination) has the same effect as a physical perception.

Francoise Dolto's contribution to the field of olfaction at the level of mother and child well illustrates the extent to which the presence of the caregiver depends on smell and smelling. This is a presence, which has a pacifying effect as well as the obvious function of meeting the baby's needs. As is apparent to anyone with clinical experience of very young children, hunger is not satisfied only by sucking on the breast or bottle: reassuring words spoken by the mother can temporarily alleviate the tension or pain caused by the hunger/thirst. Similarly, the smell of the mother's milk is a promise that hunger/thirst is about to be satisfied, and hunger/thirst are satisfied with oral drive objects (milk) to the accompaniment of the pacifying voice of the mother (lullabies, etc.), the touch and warmth of her skin, as well as her smell. So, smell can be an additional object along the path to satisfaction and can have an effect that is similar to spoken words, and can perhaps act more quickly and more intensely than words.

We can speculate here that olfactory experience acquires the status of a narrative. As mentioned above, Francoise Dolto emphasises that the mother's presence has at least two fundamental functions – physiological satisfaction and reassurance – and the smell of the mother's body, by reassuring the baby that it is being taken care of, functions as a narrative, which is not a spoken language but a property of the body (that of the mOther in Dolto's account). We may add to this the subject's own odour when, for example, the child is stained with its own bodily wastes that have a strong smell (urine, faeces, vomit and sweat). Over and above the tactile sensation of those products (the uncomfortable sensation of wetness and irritation on the skin), their smell can irritate or excite the subject. The mother's body, its warmth and her holding the baby (tactility) can reassure the young child that its demand will soon be satisfied. On the side of the subject, smell is a particularly powerful indicator suggesting that satisfaction (relief of the troubling tension/pain) is imminent, and its effect in this direction is probably greater than the sound of the mOther's voice. Dolto takes voice and smell to be objects, which function as measurement tools, enabling the baby to gauge the distance or proximity of the caregiver. There will be more to say about Dolto's contribution to the field of olfaction (Dolto, 1984).

The drive also plays out in the symbolic dimension between two human subjects (mother and child). The relation between the subject and demand (shown in Lacan's matheme as $ \lozenge D (Lacan, 1966)) happens through a communication between the subject and the mOther. This is where the first feeling of hope and fear (a tantalising feeling) is experienced. Based on what we discussed above, smell can both facilitate and accompany such feelings. Such a function is not simply part of conditional learning, which is much discussed in the field of psychology. Nor it is an imaginary vehicle in the communication between mother and child. Sniffing one's baby in order to understand its need or making sure of its comfort and well-being by following clues offered by the baby's body odour is a different kind of communication, belonging to the Imaginary register. How the mother's actions impact the child's interpretation of their meaning is an important question, which plays a pivotal role in the subject's position towards the Other. We wonder, for example, from a psychoanalytic perspective: what is the effect on a subject's formation and relationship with the other (as a social being) if a mother does not clean her baby as regularly as she should or if she comments on the child's smell. In this respect, the olfactory sense can compete with visual, tactile or vocal perceptions as a means of communicating a demand between the subject and Other and, in some cases, be more effective than them. In some cultures, perfuming the baby's body after washing or anointing the child with a natural, pleasant fragrance finalises the cleaning rituals, and the use of floral perfumed water (such as rose water) for the first few baths is a way to sanction or treasure the arrival of a new-born through an olfactory reference. We can wonder how fragrance as an added value (not an essential object to treat pain or overcome discomfort), affects the signification of the subject. Conversely, if a baby is neglected as regards its skin hygiene, or the mother herself has poor personal hygiene, what mark can the bad odour leave on the subject (assuming that it is indeed perceived as a bad odour)? Clearly, olfactory status can be highly complicated when we take each case individually and our focus is not to give a clear-cut theoretical explanation of sensual experience in a speaking being.

Moving forward in Freud's theorisation of the drive, his *Three Essays on the Theory of Sexuality* (1905) make it still clearer that the *Trieb* is not an animalistic instinct. The drive is formulated as a concept 'between' psyche and soma, a psychical representative of a bodily impulse, bridging the gap between physical impulses and the psychical representative of those impulses, which Freud had previously treated as separate. Then later, in 1915, Freud clearly considers the drive as an unconscious formation, which is not the same as the representative of the stimuli, since it cannot be manifested in consciousness. The drive is represented by an idea ('Vorstellung') and the subject has conscious access only to the 'ideational representative' of a drive:

> A drive can never become an object of consciousness – only the idea that represents the drive can. Even in the unconscious, moreover, a drive cannot be represented otherwise than by an idea ("Vorstellung"). (Freud, 1915b, p. 177; here and in Freud quotations below, I replace 'instinct' in the *Standard Edition* by 'drive' as a more accurate translation of 'Trieb').

If we try using Lacanian language to reflect upon what Freud teaches us at this stage of his conceptualisation of the drive, we might say: the drive is not an Imaginary representation of the need. The physical need of an organic body triggers an impulse to send a message to the subject, forcing them to take action in order to remove the pain (hunger, thirst, agitation, irritation, etc.). Such impulses are experienced by the subject at the conscious level. However, when a baby refuses to eat or remains agitated after being changed, the caregiver is dealing with a demand. The child itself is unaware of why it feels such discomfort and when, for example, it sucks its thumb or makes sounds in order to calm itself, we see clearly that what is at stake is not merely an organic need. The fact that a subject, implicated by an internal, organic force, either makes others take action or turns to itself to do something about the tension, reminds us of the engagement of the Other in the economy of the drive, which belongs to the realm of the Symbolic. What happens between the feeling of discomfort or tension at the level of the organic body and the course of action that takes place afterwards, both on the side of the baby and of the caregiver, can be outlined as follows: on the way from an internal tension (Real) to its representation through a conscious idea (Imaginary), a call to the mOther (Symbolic) occurs, which summons her to become engaged with this call. In other words, invoking the Other is not simply drawing their attention to a need in order to remove the urgency; the subject is actively engaged and invokes the Other to join a mutual game of enjoyment around such an urgency. As a result of such interactive engagement, the subject not only starts to form their knot of being by figuring out the meaning of their being for the Other (signification); they also fabricate and gain a form of enjoyment through the experience of needs.

The confusion around Freud's references to the drives of self-preservation and of sexuality is where Lacan re-reads the Freudian drive. Lacan's contribution to the topic of the drive invites us to reflect upon the concept as not merely a source of enjoyment but as an intrinsic part of the formation of the subject. He makes this advance by distinguishing the three concepts of need, demand and desire. The invocation addressed to the Other is not simply a matter of survival. Working with new-borns shows us the playfulness involved in communicating and meeting their essential needs. The multitude of bodily gestures, refusals to eat, holding breath, tantrums, falling asleep while eating or not sleeping, etc., cannot be interpreted simply as a survival strategy. It is true, as people say, that not every cry which a baby utters, is a cry for help. However, as is clear from work with new-borns and babies, every cry is a cry/call to the Other in the language of the drive, seeking enjoyment. What is a call? What form or shape does such a call take? And what does 'enjoyment' mean for the being of a subject?

Let us continue reading Freud closely in the light of Lacan's elaboration. Freud at this stage of his writings (the time of the First World War), refers to psychical energy (libido) and the drive. The libido comes from a drive. Five years later, in *Beyond the Pleasure Principle*, Freud himself confesses that the concept of the drive-in psychoanalysis is ambiguous. Now, he uses the term 'excitation' to describe the drive and he writes:

> The most abundant sources of this internal excitation are what are described as the organism's drives – the representatives of all the forces originating in the interior of the body and transmitted to the mental apparatus – at once the most important and the most obscure element of psychological research.
>
> (Freud, 1920, p. 34)

In this work, Freud introduces and describes the life and death drives. There is persistent confusion over the meaning of the libido, the instincts and the drives in Freud's writing. The idea of narcissism in his essay of 1914 starts with an exploration of a self-preservative libido/instinct/drive. The ego libido, which is narcissistic, is in essential contrast with the object libido. In his paper 'Drives and Their Vicissitudes' published in 1915, Freud divides the drives between the ego (or self-preservative) drives and the partial sexual drives. Freud elaborates on the four terms used in reference to the drive as: pressure, aim, object and source. Pressure is the motor force of the drive arrangement, while the source is in the living body of the subject. Freud also asserts that the object of the drive does not have to be 'extraneous': it can be a part of the subject's own body.

He introduces the four vicissitudes of the drive as follows:

1   Reversal into the opposite, which is composed of two processes: activity to passivity and the reversal of the content. The former process concerns two pairs, which are sadism-masochism and scopophilia-exhibitionism, while the latter is found in the 'transformation of love into hate.' According to Freud, this reversal impacts the *aim* of the drive.
2   Turning round upon the subject's own self: how a subject obtains pleasure from their own body.
3   Repression: treated here as one vicissitude of the drive, repression is elaborated separately by Freud in the same year in a separate paper ('Repression', 1915). Freud makes the concept of the drive into an unconscious formation as early as infancy.
4   Sublimation: by making repression into one of the drive's vicissitudes, Freud invites the reader to pose a question on the status of the satisfaction that occurs in sublimation. There are many possible ways to reach a satisfaction for each drive. (Freud, 1915a, p. 126)

We see here the beginning of Freud's dualistic approach to the concept of the drive, preparing his theorisation of the life and death drives in *Beyond the Pleasure Principle* (1920). The nature of the drive in that work is essentially sexual and the trajectory of his ideas on the drive lands on the death drive, which was elaborated in more depth in 1926 in *Civilization and its Discontents* (Freud, 1926).

Post Freudian Reading of the Drive

'… Guided by your fragrance to these charming countries,
I see a port filled with sails and rigging
Still utterly wearied by the waves of the sea,
While the perfume of the green tamarinds,
That permeates the air, and elevates my nostrils,
Is mingled in my soul with the sailors' chanteys.'
(Baudelaire, 2015, P. 41)

In the poem *Exotic Perfume*, Baudelaire describes the emotion of lust and his joyful sexual excitation by referring to the odour of his beloved's body: 'When, with both my eyes closed, on a hot autumn night, I inhale the fragrance of your warm breast, I see happy shore spread out before me …'. He travels in imagination to faraway shores, guided by her fragrance. What excited the poet was the perfume in the air of those distant lands, the odours that mingled with the songs (chanteys) of the sailors. So, enjoyment through the faculty of olfaction pairs up with an auditory enjoyment. Was it specifically the singing that invoked such an elevation of spirit or was it the perfume? Was the scent an additive value to the enjoyment experienced by the subject, or was he obtaining enjoyment purely through the invocatory and olfactory drives?

We may ask here whether the invocatory drive in a subject need to be concerned solely with the voice of the caregiver. If we focus on the specifically invocatory aspect of hearing, an invoking call that is (or is not) interpreted as an invocation by the subject can originate from registers other than the auditory faculty. It can also stem from the tactile, visual or olfactive faculties. Equally, a child might not subjectify a vocalised call as an invocation.

We learnt from Freud that civilised man has formed an arrangement of the drive, which is not the same as instinct. Lacan, in his eleventh seminar (Lacan, 1963–1964) attempts to clear up confusion in Freud's conceptualisation of the drive, by making it into a purely symbolic construction. He asserts that the concept of the drive, is 'integrated into analytic practice' just as much as the concept of the unconscious, and that the origin of both concepts is hidden. Lacan, in his own way no less than Freud, made the drive an essential part of the analytic experience, without which psychoanalysis could not come into existence. Lacan keeps the four Freudian elements of the drive: pressure, source, object and aim. He also accepts Freud's statement that the drive belongs to the subject's 'myth', but replaces the word 'myth' by 'fiction' as a more faithful equivalent to Freud's use of the word 'convention'. According to Lacan, the Freudian conceptualisation of the drive-in terms of internal force/urges, with roots in physiology as well as physics, amounts to a fundamental personal fiction. In other words, travelling from the Real of the organism to the Symbolic personal myth, the drive is shaped at the heart of human sexuality and offers enjoyment to the subject based on an unconscious scenario (the fantasy). A drive arrangement is detectable in every symptom that is presented in the analytic work. The function of the drive in the symptom is to offer a subject a mode of enjoyment, which makes the symptom maximally sustainable. The fantasy, as a bridge between the drive and symptom, is the fiction that each individual concocts based on the physical internal urges or excitations, which they experience as early as infancy, and on the handling of those demands through communication with the caregiver as the first significant Other.

In Seminar 11, Lacan goes on to remark on another primitive function of the drive, which is to allow subjects to distinguish their internal being from the external world. He develops his theorisation through a consideration of internal needs, such as thirst and hunger, and the way in which they are handled by the Other. As Freud emphasised, those urges are constant in their nature (they are a 'constant force'). Freud's point, according to Lacan, was that the drive cannot be regulated. Topologically speaking, the drive is ceaseless and has non-no clear-cut start and end point to its movement. Other internal sensations, such as the experience of an unpleasant degree of hot or cold, pressure, roughness or weight on skin or strong irritating odours, can be added to the primitive internal sensations of hunger and thirst, which Freud adduced. Returning now to the question of enjoyment, Lacan, like Freud, sees the drive and satisfaction as two opposite notions. The drive never obtains full satisfaction by reaching its object. True to Freud's understanding of satisfaction, as highlighted in *Beyond the Pleasure Principle*, Lacan says that 'the pleasure of the mouth' will never be achieved by means of food, the hallucination of the food or the mother's care, but specifically by the breast. Lacan writes ironically of 'ordering a menu' for the oral drive: there is no food, which can fully satisfy the 'hunger' of the oral drive, as illustrated by the endless innovations of the food industry, food advertising and the complexity of food politics as demonstrated by Michelin stars and menu creation. The breast, which is what is really at issue in 'the pleasure of the mouth' stands for the *object little a* – the cause of the subject's desire. This object makes the drive circuit turn around itself, tricking the Real of sexuality (Lacan uses the French word 'tour', which has the double meaning of 'turning' and 'tricking'). This Lacanian reading of the Freudian invention allows smell to be understood as the object cause of desire, which generates a sense of reassurance for the infant of being loved, cared for and held by the caregiver. The testimony of analytic practice witnesses that the olfactory drive generates sexual pleasure and manifests itself in the obsession of certain subjects with pleasant or unpleasant odours, perfume shopping, and even the choice of a life partner based on their smell or belief in the power of pheromones. As regards the source of the drive in so called 'erogenous zones', Lacan refers specifically to the anal drive and says that the function of excrement is a form of exchange with the external world. Human excrement has a strong odour and we can think of the source of the olfactory drive as the nose, receiving the object of smell from one's own body as well as the body of the other. In the anal drive, faeces is an exchange with the other, where the subject's excrement is the object of exchange, while the smell can be involved in exchange between the subject and the other, which goes either way: to or from the subject or the other.

As can be seen, the drive is among the most problematic concepts in psychoanalysis. Moving away now from our critical reading of this concept, we can ask: would it be possible and useful to draw boundary lines between each faculty of the drive when we elaborate the gain of enjoyment from each drive montage from a psychoanalytic perspective? What consequences could the idea of a distinction between each faculty of the drive have in clinical work?

We may find it difficult, when elaborating the domain of each drive from a psychoanalytic point of view, to draw a clear-cut boundary between them. At the level of individual enjoyment, two or more arrangements of the drives can share or impact experience by complementing, diminishing or distorting the nature and intensity of excitation. For instance, olfaction can influence the scopic and invocatory registers. It can function as a complementary add-on to the enjoyment gained through the other two drives. Examples at the level of everyday life experience include smelling a pleasant scent when listening to music, enjoying the fragrance of flowers while looking at a landscape, or enjoying the smell of food while listening to or watching some entertainment. Identifying the subject's access to the enjoyment gained from various drive montages is a complex task. The work of differentiation is also complex in the clinical handling of some sexual practices, which involve sexual pleasure obtained from the malodorous body of the sexual partner or even their bodily waste while touching them or watching them engaged in a sexual act (the tactile and the scopic drives). The principal question in the clinic is the mode of enjoyment and the direction of analytic experience is not greatly dependent on such a differentiating approach at the level of drive montage. Moreover, as is a common experience for many analysands, olfactory input has the power to obstruct or change the entirety of scopic or invocatory enjoyment. A pleasant visual appearance can cause repulsion when it is linked to a stench.

Reference to cinema might help to clarify the discussion at this point. In the South Korean film *Parasite* (2019), odour takes the leading role, relegating the power of the visual image to second place. This dark comedy-thriller, directed by Bong Joon-ho, focused on the social class divisions in contemporary South Korean society through a pronounced reference to olfaction. From the stench of bodily waste (sweat, excrement, etc.) to the odours of fragrant scents and cleanliness, the film was designed to depict the marker of smell through visual representations. The director uses facial expressions, body language and mimicry, deepening or holding the breath, the oral narratives of characters and the sound of the film score to elicit odours, pleasant and unpleasant, in the minds of viewers. At a climax point in the film, odour also acts as a signifier: one character expresses disgust at a foul smell, which is a marker of poverty, evoking such fury in another character that a murder (a 'passage to the act') is committed. Did the disgusting smell cause an unconscious pulsation that allowed a desire to be articulated? Or was it the object of the drive?

In another sequence from the same film, amid dramatic scenes of a flooding sewer, we see how the stench of poverty, as represented by this scene, creates far less concern among the film's characters than more urgent and serious worries such as homelessness and hunger. We are shown too how the smell of sweat exuded by the male protagonist becomes the main point of resentment against his role of labourer for a wealthy boss. Disgust, which is usually elaborated at the level of the oral drive, cannot really be considered separately from the olfactory plane, and odours, as the object of the olfactory drive, create a narrative that generates a mode of enjoyment no less than a piece of music or a work of visual art. One may also wonder about the power of odours when a subject's unconscious interpretation of an olfactory input supports and sustains his or her desire (forming a symptom) or their way of enjoying themselves as a sexed being. This issue will be approached in the last chapter when we discuss how odours have an effect on the formation of our sexed and social being.

Also relevant to the invocatory plane, clinical cases are not uncommon where the subject makes him- or herself 'heard' through the object of olfaction, either by having a smelly body or through an obsessive attempt at deodorising and re-odorising in order to invoke the Other. Historically, in the psychoanalytic literature, such clinical manifestations around dirt and cleanliness have been considered in the context of the anal drive. But further elaboration of such narratives in the clinic often reveals that the issue is not so much the withholding or release/emptying out of faeces or other bodily excrements (the object of the anal drive), as a concern over bodily or environmental smell. Such strong, symbolic olfactory references in a subject's narrative (smelling like dirt or covering the body with perfume) can be a way of orienting the person's life around specific rituals and values in order to give substance to their being (as happens in psychotic structure) or may play a role in forming a symptom (in neurotic structure). Obsession with a particular smell is also a common manifestation of perversion.

Freud believed that a foot fetish is the result of a 'partial repression'. He writes to Karl Abraham on 18th February 1909 that in cases of foot fetishism, the foot and its foul smell are a unit, but while the 'original olfactory pleasure' is repressed, the other part (the foot) is 'idealised'. He finds an exact parallel to this development in clothes fetishism:

> I also know clothes fetishists, in whom the connection is even closer. They are former voyeurs, watchers of undressing scenes, for whom clothes were

once very much in the way. The normal clothes fetishism of women is also connected with the passive drive to be seen, with exhibitionism.

(Abraham, 2002, P. 83)

So, just as for the clothes fetishist the true object is the naked body, so for the foot fetishist the olfactory pleasure is what is original and repressed. Another register of the drive (scopic) replaces the olfactory pleasure, but the olfactory pleasure is primitive, original, and fundamental to the subject, and its repression is surely a means of its preservation.

Other first-generation analysts, Ernest Jones and Sandor Ferenczi, both followed Freud's anal drive theory when exploring odours and olfaction in their clinical cases.

As human civilization evolved, olfaction remained the most intimate sense because the very first subjective distinction of one's being from the Other's happens through olfactory experience. This can be observed in clinical work with new-borns and babies and it is the reason why Françoise Dolto suggested that a child who is parted from its mother and refuses to drink milk or fall asleep should be given a piece of the mother's clothing, which retains the mother's body odour. As mentioned earlier, for Dolto, the mother's body is recognised by the infant via two main senses: smell and voice. The smell signals the proximity of the mother for the child and her voice signals her distance. Hearing and smell are the two media by which a new-born begins to acquire a sense of space and of the body – its own and that of its mother. So, the absence or presence of one's own being and that of the other are recognised and distinguished long before the field of vision comes into play. Moreover, if we compare the two registers, smelling and hearing, we find that the object of smell disappears/evaporates more quickly than the voice. So, the sense of smell is the quickest marker of the absence of the care giver when she leaves the vicinity of the young child. And, conversely, it is often the first sign of her proximity when she returns. Here, we must be careful not to take the object of olfaction – smell – merely as a medium for recognising the other as distinct from the self. As we will see, this recognition is always accompanied by a sense of reassurance. It is a matter of feeling safe or being held as a social and sexed subject who is born into a narrative, containing the structure of law or, in other words, being born at the beginning of an unknown path that the child either wants or does not want to embark upon. The narrative can manifest itself in both spoken and unspoken languages.

Dolto reminds us that the smell of the mother's body is reassuring to the infant. What does such a reassurance amount to as regards other objects of the drives, such as the mother's skin? Would it not be more logical to think that being safely held (an aspect of the tactile drive) is more important for reassurance than the smell of the skin? Babies are held by other members of family and by friends, and the child must sense their smells, but the smell of its mother/primary caregiver stands out from the others. Dolto's clinical case of a three-day-old baby girl during the Second World War shows us clearly how much depends on the olfactory object, rather than a loving touch, to make the baby feel safe and cared for. The infant refused to eat, despite showing no signs of sadness or agitation, but was able to do so once her mother's night-gown was placed next to her. Dolto's interpretation of the case was centred on the child's regression to an earlier stage of life, in the mother's womb, where the child definitely felt safe. We may wonder, though, about the assumption that being carried in the womb is the ultimate sensation of safety. Could the womb not also be felt as an unsafe environment when, for example, the odour/taste of food consumed or the respiratory movements of the mother disrupt the serenity of the child in the womb? Although we agree with Dolto's remarks on the significance of olfaction in providing safety and reassurance for the subject, there are surely other ways of interpreting what she describes in the case of the new-born and the mother's gown. Might we not see it as an act of regression or the expression of a death wish? Could it be that what was impor-tant for the child in this case was simply to force other people to take action (to bring her the gown)?

Psychoanalysis and the Complexity of Olfaction

The last question I want to ask in this chapter is whether smell is best defined as a drive and whether we should treat it as such in the clinical materials?

Celine Sciamma's film fantasy, *Petite Maman* (2021), portrays a mother-and-daughter relationship. In one scene, the eight-year-old Nelly expresses her grief over her grandmother's death to another young child, Marion (who is, in fact, her own mother). Nelly lights on her grandmother's stick as the principal memento of the deceased, because its smell establishes a direct link with and evokes her grandmother's presence. So, an odour, rather than any specific tangible object, is the most fundamental link with a loved one who has died – a living trace of someone who is no longer among the living. In-deed, what is effectively in play here is surely the odour of the living body of the girl's grandmother. It is often true that the smell of a person who was close to us – evoked by the smell of an object that they kept close to their body when they were alive or simply by our olfactory memory – is what produces the most vivid sense of their presence after their departure. In this case smell gives a glimpse of a lived experience (bodily excitation), and the mechanism can be understood under the auspices of drive theory. But the mechanism is also reminiscent of what happens in the formation of the subject through the processes of alienation and separation, and we might conjecture that the highlighting of an odour as a link with the deceased amounts to a regression to those processes. Firstly, there is recognition of the caregiver's bodily odour (alienation) and then, secondly, the making of a distinction between the odour of one's own body and the odour of the Other's body (separation). Smell, to a greater degree than warmth and the voice of the caregiver, is what is most intimate and primitive between child and carer. It is felt at a shorter distance than voice and touch.

It is not uncommon to hear in the clinic of occasions when a garment (as an object close to the body) or a bottle of the perfume of someone, whom the patient has lost or been separated from, is kept as a memento or representation of their presence. It is not the warmth, touch or look of the loved one, which has imparted a particular meaning to the garment. Rather, it is the smell of the body that has marked the presence or liveliness of the person in question. Even long after the odour has faded to nothing, the item remains the container of the smell and we might say that olfactory perception is under the rule of metaphor. Souvenirs and mementos of somebody who has been lost can operate at the level of the scopic drive and imagination if, for example, we imagine seeing the person in particular clothes. Or memento objects may invoke the invocatory drive, as in the case of a piece of music. But, in practice, none of these objects can compete with the effect of olfaction on the subject in terms of depth and the speed at which the invoking effect works at the level of emotions and feelings. The very act of inhaling the familiar smell of the lost one is an intimate practice consisting of an active, voluntary plane (breathing in), which happens inside the body, and the passive plane of being catapulted to another time and another state of feeling and emotion. In such a practice, the excitement (whether joy or desperation) that is felt upon sensing the smell is sought for over and over again, each time aiming to bring lost presence to life. In the example from Sciamma's film, the instrument of the experience was a personal belonging, which referenced an olfactory object, but in many cases of grief it may be the smell of a particular place or time of the year, which brings the memory of the lost one intensely and immediately back to the grieving subject. It is a common and familiar experience that no image or sound can bring the lost one back to life in the way that a smell can. As Freud reminded us, in humans, the drive is not merely an ego property (instinct), which preserves the subject's life as is the case in other animals. Smell is to be understood as a sex drive in the Freudian sense, with all the characteristics, which Freud ascribed to this category and which were preserved in Lacan's work.

In the cases that have been discussed so far, the subject looks actively for the marks of an absence by the use of smell. But this may happen in a way that is involuntary, and olfactory references can come to the fore as the key clinical materials in a way that is very surprising for the analysand. In one clinical case where grief for her deceased mother was placing a heavy burden on the everyday life of a woman analysand, all the daily chores of the subject were focused on how to keep her environment odour free. This was in contrast with many grieving subjects who attempt to preserve an olfactory reference to the lost one. In this case, the main focus of the woman's symptomatic, repetitive rituals was to eliminate any malodour from her own body and the space that she had inhabited with her mother. She wanted to prevent her mother's presence (after her death) from lingering there and, in order to achieve this, any possible olfactory references that had been experienced when her mother was alive had to be got rid of. She was an obsessional cleaner and felt compelled to shower or wash her hands several times a day. In the work, when it became clearer that the mother's body was equated with her own body and that smell was the principal signifier of her mother's presence (memory of the smell of her mother's body or any other smell that reminded the subject of her, such as cooking, perfume, old furniture, etc.), we investigated why de-odorising had become her symptom since, in contrast with many grieving subjects who look for olfactory references to restore the experience of the lost one's presence, elimination of smell was the principal way in which she warded off the anguish associated with her mother's demise.

The root of her symptom was in the olfactory drive. Through investigating her past history, she came to believe that her way of dealing with loss was to obsessively eliminate a strong allusion to the love object. She also made an association with her mother's obsession with smell. Her mother had been an avid collector of perfumes, which she treated as a marker of female seduction, and this had created a strong link for the analysand between perfume and the rivalry she had experienced as a woman with her mother. She then interpreted the use of pleasant odours as a masquerade, concealing the 'holes' and 'decay' of the sexual body. She had had a conflicted relationship with her mother since her teenage years and was convinced that her mother was unable to live without the sexual attention of her serial lovers. The analysand had been wary of introducing her boyfriends to her mother for this reason, and her fear and insecurity at not being able to compete with her mother as the object of men's sexual desire or/and love had found expression in an obsession with plainness in her feminine appearance including, specifically, refusal to use any perfume or deodorant (in complete contrast with her mother's feminine position). She remembered the spray of a strong-smelling perfume as a 'final touch' in her mother's make-up rituals before she went out, and the signifier of 'final touch' then opened up a new path for the subject in exploring and tracing the arrangement of her olfactory drive and its connection with tactility. She struggled to reach orgasm, her smell obsession was a source of distress in her sex life and, in sexual relations with her husband, she experienced hyper-sensitivity on her skin when she was touched. In this context, I posed 'the final touch' to her as 'the final touch of what?'. She then stated that her access to enjoyment in life was disturbed by the fantasy of her mother as the most seductive woman, who had the attention of all men. In the scenario of her fantasy, the strong olfactory reference was the 'last nail in the coffin', by which her mother captured the gaze, invocation and touch of her lovers. Her mother's 'final touch' was the destiny touch that defined her femininity, marking her power of undisputable presence.

The analysand blamed her mother's promiscuity for her own inhibitions on sexual gratification, which was associated by her with smell. The radical equation between her mother and the olfactory object was challenged in the analysis and her obsession with eliminating smell led to themes of violence, intrusion and fierceness, all associated with the power of smell. She went so far as to compare smell with a 'rapist' – an intruder, who must be destroyed. This final breakthrough was followed by a depressive mood, where her obsession with eliminating odours waned, but her difficulty reaching orgasm was replaced by vulvodynia – a painful condition in her genitalia and anal area. She found it increasingly difficult to eat and a mild phobia of swelling appeared as a new symptomatic manifestation. She analysed the new development as a rejection of any invasion/intrusion into her body and spoke of her feelings of rage and sorrow in terms of her body (the seat of the drive montage), localising them around oral and anal drives. The investigation of these themes of hate and violence in the analysis facilitated the construction of a new interpretation around her feminine position. A few months after producing this new narrative, she had a sense of restoration of her childhood body and of herself as a 'child woman' possessing a 'virgin' and 'impenetrable' body. After passing through this final step of analysis, she found herself much less afflicted with pain and suffering.

What is clear from this clinical vignette is the complexity of the clinical presentation of the drive montage, in this case the olfactory drive, when we approach a narrative where drive references have a pronounced presence. The way in which the analysand moved from grief and obsession connected with smell to a new narrative of her mode of being as a woman suggests a link between the drive, symptom and fantasy, where the drive operates as a bridge between the latter two; and it also shows how such a link can represent the subject's sexuality. In the clinic of psychoanalysis, making a distinction between the different faculties of the drives would be futile unless the drive element guides the work towards understanding the mode of enjoyment that each subject gains from being alive and from their sexed being (in Lacanian terms, respectively, 'phallic jouissance' and 'Other jouissance'). In the case that was described above, recognising olfaction as a drive and not a signifier enabled the analysis to speak to the body rather than creating any unnecessary diversion in the treatment. Our way of treating the clinical materials for the purpose of intervention and interpretation needs to recognise the agency of the subject in forming a signification of their being, which can never exclude the body. Lacan insists that the body seeks pleasure independently, and the drive montage is one possible way to understand such a search for enjoyment.

Conclusion

We want to conclude here that olfactory references in the clinic of psychoanalysis do not necessarily have to be theorised under the auspices of the drive concept (the olfactory drive). In the example of the female analysand, discussed above, the drive, as conceptualised in the psychoanalytic literature, is not what links the subjective narrative around the meaning of her being with her mortal, sexualised body.

Another example, from modern literature, demonstrates the possibility of a radical link between olfaction, the meaning of the body, subjectivity and the symptom, which makes being coherent while offering a mode of enjoyment to the subject. In the film *Perfume: The Story of a Murderer*, based on Patrick Süskind's novel of the same name, the hero-villain and supremely talented blender of perfumes, Jean-Baptiste Grenouille, spends some time in complete isolation and realises that his own body produces no smell. The anguish and fear of oblivion, which this arouses, drives him towards madness. To smell for him is the same as to exist and not having his own smell signifies his mortality, though not necessarily his actual death. To smell is to anchored in language and not to vanish into oblivion. Here again, we see that smell and olfaction are not simply a drive montage that offers enjoyment. The imperative of having a proper smell, to smell/be smelled, drives Grenouille to extract odours from others (women) and to make a potion/perfume that gives him a scent, which is irresistible to others. Grenouille was abandoned as a child and to become 'the thing' (Freud's 'das Ding') was his solution (a perverse solution) for coming to terms with his lack as a deprivation. It is a solution, which is always equated with the problem, and it ultimately and inevitably consumes him (literally, in the final scene of the novel).

Grenouille's olfactory drive is a manifestation of the death drive and its excessive nature is repeated in every murder he commits. Olfaction here can be read and understood in very many different ways: it carries the meaning of mortal being (being forgotten), a symptom (the Lacanian 'sinthome') and the ego (equated with the 'sinthome') in the making of the potion, as well as being represented as a drive montage with a repetitive, destructive nature circulating around the *object a*, depicted in Grenouille's murders of women with deliciously scented skins. Was it not also the exciting enjoyment, or jouissance, which thrilled him with the scent of women? The scented skin of women can also be understood as the semblance of the object, around which the drive circulates. As can be seen, the reduction of human olfactory sense perception to the psychoanalytical concept of the drive will leave us with more questions and complications.

The olfactory object here follows a plot: from *how to be loved* to *how to be "the love"* to the extent that, in this story, the main protagonist was not Grenouille, but smell. A rejected child from birth (if not before his conception), his supernaturally powerful olfactory sensory faculty allows him to concoct a story of his being: as a perfumier of extraordinary skill, he eventually succeeds in fabricating the ultimate elixir of pleasure and desire. He relegates the Other to being no more than a partial object of olfaction, a portion of the ultimate elixir, which he aspires to create and eventually creates. He needed society in order to nourish such a perverse act. This is well depicted in the scene where, in his solitude, he realised that was odourless: an empty shell.

What he obtained from others was not merely the flavour of life – his very own life itself was to be recognised through smells taken from others. Now, beyond his mortal body, his potion of lust was the *object a*. To be this object, he pours the potion on himself and is devoured by others when he becomes the most desirable one, the ultimate object of love. From radical rejection to radical desire, he remains nothing more than an olfactory object.

Smell is a powerful transporter to the past, an indicator of sanity, an artistic construction for seduction and lust, or a means to access the thrill of life, it is a *sine qua non* of our formation as a speaking, mortal being, and plays an essential role in weaving our knot of being. It cannot simply remain in the drive register. It dissolves the borders between theories, true to its own irresistibly penetrative nature.

Bibliography

Abraham, K. (2002). *The Complete Correspondences of Sigmund Freud & Karl Abraham 1907–1925*. London: Routledge

Baudelaire, C. (2015). *The Flowers of the Evil, Les Fleurs Du Mal*, English and French Edition, William Ageller (Trans). Digireads Publishing

Dolto, F. (1984). *L'Image Inconsciente Du Corps*. Paris: Seuil

Freud, S. (1895). Project for Scientific Psychology, pp. 281–391. In: J. Strachey, ed. *The Standard Edition of the Complete Psychological Works of Sigmund Freud*, Vol 1. London: Vintage, 2001

Freud, S. (1905). Three Essays on the Theory of Sexuality, pp. 125–249. In: J. Strachey, ed. *The Standard Edition of the Complete Psychological Works of Sigmund Freud*, Vol. VII. London: Vintage

Freud, S. (1915a). Drives and Their Vicissitudes. pp. 109–141. In: J. Strachey, ed. *The Standard Edition of the Complete Psychological Works of Sigmund Freud*, Vol. XIV. London: Vintage, 2001

Freud, S. (1915b). The Unconscious. pp. 159–215. In: J. Strachey, ed. *The Standard Edition of the Complete Psychological Works of Sigmund Freud*, Vol. XIV. London: Vintage, 2001

Freud, S. (1920). Beyond the Pleasure Principle, pp. 7–64. In: J. Strachey, ed. *The Standard Edition of the Complete Psychological Works of Sigmund Freud*, Vol. XVIII. London: Vintage

Freud, S. (1926). Civilization and Its Discontents, pp. 57–147. In: J. Strachey, ed. *The Standard Edition of the Complete Psychological Works of Sigmund Freud*, Vol. XXI. London: Vintage

Lacan, J. (1963–1964). *The Seminar of Jacques Lacan: Book XI: The Four Fundamental Concepts of Psychoanalysis*. Alan Sheridan (Trans). New York & London: Norton

Lacan, J. (1966). *Écrits: The Subversion of the Subject and the Dialectic of Desire in the Freudian Unconscious*. pp. 671–702. Fink, B. (Trans.). The United States: Norton

Chapter 5

Breath of Life, Kiss of Death

On Breathing, the Nose and Olfaction

Introduction

Smelling is inseparable from the act of breathing. Olfaction cannot exist without respiration, on which our survival from moment to moment depends. The breathing in and out of air, whether fragrant (giving pleasure to the subject) or foul (perhaps hazardous for health), gives meaning to the border of our being through a simple but foundational structure. The contrast of inside and outside is felt constantly, continuously and unconsciously. The tactile, scopic and invocatory faculties, unlike olfaction (and also taste), do not distinguish the inside and outside of our body, but only show the outer border of our body as distinct from its surroundings. Breathing and hence smelling is exceptional because they enter and exit the body without conscious awareness. We can control what we smell only by controlling our breathing. We breathe in smells that are unwelcome and can only stop their inflow by holding our breath or breathing through our mouth, neither of which is sustainable for long. A patient of mine with severe obsessional rituals related to cleanliness and dirt told me that she held her breath in public toilets and when standing close to others. Her aversion was not to foul odour, but rather to the bodily waste of others, as if that object was equated with its smell and breathing was a conduit, through which it might enter her body.

The air we breathe is always scented. We usually get used to new smells quickly and stop noticing them, but our first breath in every new space that we enter comes with a particular smell. When we arrive in a new city, the smell of the air establishes its character and gives us new markers of space and time before we can make sense of its sights and sounds.

Our living being, which depends from moment to moment on breathing, is essentially marked by language and this fact gives other dimensions to the act of breathing. In religions and in literature breathing has been accorded a status beyond its physiological essentiality. In Judaism and Christianity, smell and breath play an important role in portraying and making the distinction between heaven and hell and, more generally, between what is pleasant and what is unpleasant. The common motif is that a sweet smell is pleasant and is

DOI: 10.4324/9781003485322-5

also healing or sacred. Religions forge links between the breath of God and the human soul. In the biblical account, human beings came into existence out of the dust and were given life by God's breath – the breath of life into man's nostrils.

Breathing is living and claiming life. It is intimate: lovers breathe each other's air. The language of breathing is sexualised, and yet it is associated with a higher being. Respiration and hence smell are woven into our descriptions of our lived experience to an extent that would often surprise us if pointed out – the words of our descriptions become 'smelly'. From the bad breath of the devil to the sweet breath of a lover, our speaking being is marked by breathing. One of the ultimate expressions found and used in the language of lovers is to be each other's breath – a radical reference to mutual dependence – and intimacy is marked by breathing and tolerating each other's bodily odours. Narratives around the first signs of love or on the contrary, the impossibility of intimacy with someone, are often enriched with references to breathing the air or smell of the other subject.

We breathe each other's air and this gives air (and odour) a unique quality compared to the other objects on the drives. Our shared yet individual dependence of the air around us makes breathing almost a competitive activity. In the Imaginary register, we make sense of our organic survival based on the air we take in. Breathing is living and as we strive to live, we can find ourselves in competition with others. The first dyadic contrast with the other for an infant subject happens at birth, when it has to breathe independently of its mother's body. Certainly, the body of the new-born has to claim life in other ways as well, but breathing is surely the most radical change that occurs after birth compared with life in the womb. Breathing, as the key difference between life inside and outside the womb, can also be read as the first marker of freedom. The new-born child must still address its organic needs to the mOther, but the acquisition of language with all its layers and properties, starts with the independent breathing of air. So, breathing opens a door to the matrix of complex communication and trading with the Other of body and language, involving both freedom and dependence.

In this chapter, we will be elaborating the most fundamental aspect of olfaction, which is breathing, through the lens of psychoanalysis. What does breathing really mean for our living being, which is both mortal and sexualised? How are we marked by the language of breathing and vice-versa, how is our breathing marked by the signifier?

First Breath

In human beings, the first breath is simultaneous and identical with the first cry. The sound of air opening millions of air sacs in the lungs is the baby's cry for life, and this coincidence of sound and respiration also coincides with the first olfactory experience as the inhaled air brings with it the first scent. Air penetrates the body before the body begins to ingest food, and brings with it an odour – the olfactory object. As breathing proceeds autonomously, the young child is exposed to a diverse range of odours, both pleasant and unpleasant. We might think of this division between fragrance and stench as the way in which a new-born perceives and interprets qualities prior to the acquisition of the language. Olfaction is the first tool for recognising people, food and places, when vision is not yet fully developed. As the new-born breathes in and out, odour is a companion to the vital air, so that vitality is bound up with the presence of odours. The meaning of otherness prior to any visualisation of the other (of the non-self) also depends on olfactory experience. A subject breathes in the other and steps into life (both organically and psychically) before seeing themselves in the mirror in the presence of the other who speaks of the child's appearance. So, the beginnings of subjective formation come with olfactory experience of the other and predate the Lacanian conceptualisation of the mirror phase. It is thought-provoking that in most cultures there are more sayings around a child's appearance than around its smell: olfactory perception has a silent presence in language compared with visual input. Many commentators (including Havelock Ellis) have speculated that this could be a fairly recent development, as if human smell has become unaesthetic in the modern world. The smell of the subject and other at the level of the mother-and-child relationship was elaborated in the previous chapter. Here, we want to emphasise breathing as an autonomous act, from which olfaction is inseparable. Later in life, a subject can control their breathing in order to avoid a strong odour, a stench or a particular scent. In infancy, however, olfactory experience happens to the subject involuntarily as it breathes air in order to survive.

Ernest Jones wrote about breathing and olfaction in a paper, which can be found in the second volume of his *Essays in Applied Psychoanalysis*. Referring to biblical accounts of the act of breathing, he highlights the connections made in the Bible between the act of breathing and fertilisation (Mary's impregnation by the breath of Gabriel) and the story in the Old Testament of the creation of man out of dust, where God breathes into man's nostrils to make him into 'a living soul' (Jones, 1951, p. 274). Jones elaborates the act of breathing on two planes: orality (breathing and speaking) and anality (the emission of air from the body). Equating breathing with the symbol of life and noting that absence of breath is the most basic test for death, Jones emphasises what he calls the 'mysterious invisibility' of this act. The same is also true for smell: it is invisible and therefore mysterious. However, Jones believes that the act of breathing has much less of a role in the formation of unconscious ideas compared with the emission of air from the body. Breathing, like heart-beat, is automatic, so the subject does not pay attention to it or show any interest in it. For Jones, it is 'excreted air' (flatulence) which, becomes associated with various affects and ideas in later life. The smelly air that issues from the intestines contributes to the formation of unconscious phantasies and other mental formations. He notes the identification between intestinal gas and sexual excretion in a reproduction phantasy that is common among children, whereby the flatulent gas/air from the father is what impregnates the mother. Jones refers to odour as just one of five attributes of the air that is emitted from the body (through either flatulence or eructation). His list of attributes is thought-provoking in relation to the various types of drive, which have been described in psychoanalysis. This list includes blowing movement (anal drive), sound (invocatory drive), invisibility (scopic drive), moisture, warmth (tactile drive) and lastly odour (olfactory drive) (Jones, 1951, p. 279). Jones applies his list to psychoanalytic accounts of unconscious phantasies and ideas around birth.

For Jones, then, it is not only the air that is breathed in and out, but specific characteristics of the wind emitted from the body, which mark the inception of a subject. In Jones' conceptualisation the subject takes breathing for granted as part of organic life, while mental life and phantasy stem from a 'wind of life'! Discussing the connection between wind and the 'fertilising principle' he refers to both Greek mythology and the mythology of the Algonkin people in North America, both of which associate wind/air with the concept of fertility. In the Greek myth, Hera, the goddess of marriage and protector of women during childbirth, conceived Hephaestus by the wind, without union with Zeus (there are other versions of the story of Hera's impregnation with Hephaestus, but Jones picks the version, which makes the wind into the fertilizer). He gives more examples from ancient philosophy (Aristotle and Pliny) and the myths of various peoples, which ascribe fertilising qualities to the wind, and shows how the power of wind/air is elevated from a source of life, birth and creation to something akin to life itself or the essence of God. Air as an agent of birth and creation is transformed into the sacred breath of God, as if God is poured into the body of the subject with the power of turning him/her into a living and sexualised being.

Breath, then, is associated with mortality (the power of life and birth/rebirth) and sexuality (inhaling magical air with fertilising power) as well as the soul and joy of being in a human subject. Is the first breath not a claim to life? Can we not see the infant's first breath as the first step to independence from the caregiver, away from the dependence implied by the other essential needs, such as food, touch, warmth? This makes breathing a particular action of the subject, an assertion of individuality. Unlike sucking, defecation is the need to be held and kept warm or to hear the reassuring sound of the caregiver near at hand, all of which call for the involvement of the Other, breathing happens autonomously and independently after birth. It does not call for the Other's intervention. The new-born has to claim life with his or her first breath. What does this mean for the subject on the way to coming into being? In which way can the act of breathing, as an independent act intertwined with olfaction, mark the significance of the body (the Real body), the liveliness of a subject, his or her access to the enjoyment of the drive montage and the formation of the first desire (being loved/wanted)?

At least, such thoughts and questions make it unsurprising that we find breath described as the ultimate form of shared life ('being each other's breath') in poetic literature devoted to love and intimacy. Disgust at the odours of each other's bodies, including the smell of each other's breath, is usually far from the thoughts of lovers. In the language of poetry, statements such as 'you are the air I breathe' or 'you are my breath' not only express the sense of being alive and the dependence between lover and beloved; they capture the extent and depth of connection between the couple, where the absence of boundary or of selfhood apart from the beloved is a key feature. Being 'blind for love' suggests an intimate connection between rationality and the visual faculty, both of which are obscured by love. But breath and olfaction take the level of intimacy and loss of boundaries to a whole new level. As was already discussed, olfaction, through its close relationship with breath, is the only sensory faculty, which travels to the inner body (the Imaginary body), changes the subjective interpretation and significance beyond what can be imparted by a look or touch (the Symbolic body) and leaves the subject with an uncanny sensation or a particular excitation that is beyond any symbolic meaning (the Real body).

Having agreed that the first breath is both an organic and a symbolic event, we then need to ask what happens around the new-born's first experience of inhaling odorous air, which can leave an invisible mark on the Real being of the subject to be. This is a bodily event and any interruption or obstruction of breathing at the level of the organic body, and the way in which such situations are handled by the medical team or the mother, can have an impact on a subject's mode of being. The presence and resonance of events around the first breath at the level of the caregiver's narrative (and the narrative told by others) can also mark a subject. Such invisible marks are not necessarily focused on the airways of the body or the respiratory system as a whole: they can be manifest at the level of the olfactory faculty. In one clinical vignette, a mother of a three-month young baby consulted me a few years ago with concerns about the possibility of autism in her child. She held her child during the consultation. This mother had previously given birth to a child who had shown clear signs of autism since early infancy. The mother herself suffered from asthma attacks and both her first and second labours had been difficult. She had then developed a postpartum depression and a worrying insomnia after the birth of her first child. She recounted that sleepless nights and asthma attacks in the early mornings were triggered by a phobia of being choked/unable to breathe in her sleep. She had received various treatments, but the phobia was still present. Her second pregnancy was also difficult and the prolonged labour had led to an obstruction in the baby's airways, causing amniotic aspiration. The baby was in an incubator for the first couple of days after the birth. What made the mother seek consultation concerning autism in her second child was the child's refusal to suck at the breast and some brief episodes of breath-holding just before the time of our first meeting. During the consultation, the baby girl was quiet but attentive to certain movements of the mother and to the mother's speech: when the mother made reference specifically to her, she moved or looked at me or her mother.

The mother's symptom, which was localised around her respiratory system, had found a means of expression in both of her children. The first was diagnosed with reactive airways and the second had developed breath-holding episodes, which, together with the eating/sucking avoidance, indicated a definite agency on the part of the young child. It became evident that such episodes occurred when the mother herself was agitated due to her insomnia or the asthma attacks or due to the side-effects of her medication. Maternal guilt also played a significant role in this case, particularly in the mother's narrative around her prolonged labour that had caused respiratory distress for her child. She was made anxious by thoughts of how her difficulties in becoming a mother might have affected her children's health. This narrative had a strong presence in her daily conversations with others and was mentioned as early as our first meeting: she associated the possibility of autism in the children with the distress they had suffered at birth. After our first meeting, she decided to continue the analytic work herself, but wanted to focus the work around her children. As the work continued, we spent much time exploring materials related to breathing. She first suffered from asthma as a teenager when she used a great deal of perfume with intense scents. She had developed an obsessive avoidance of bad odours around that time and her indulgence in perfume was her way of suppressing any such odours. Her own mother had suffered from halitosis and her skin had emitted a strong acidic scent in stressful situations. The analysand had little to say about her mother, other than negative references to her odour problems, as if her mother was represented only by her halitosis – she was 'the smell'. It also emerged that the bad smell was a marker of weakness and poverty for the analysand, and this was an association that she had made since childhood. At the same time, she felt guilt at having such emotions and thoughts in respect of her mother. She interpreted her overuse of perfume as a way of covering up what she most feared, which was to be called 'stinky'. She had heard this offensive expression used many times by her father about her mother.

The analysand's mother had a reputation for holding grudges against anyone she perceived as having behaved unfairly towards her and the analysand once said in a session that her mother was 'the bad breath', meaning that her bodily odours were an expression of her death wishes against those who had hurt her. This led back to her own maternal guilt. Her idea that her children's breathing-related symptoms were due to her difficulties in pregnancy and labour amounted to a belief that a 'stinky curse' had been cast on the breath of the next generation of her family. The emphasis here was very much on the maternal line: in her narrative, her father's bad breath (he was alcoholic) was dismissed, but his derogatory words about the mother's bad odour were blamed for causing misery. The expression 'bad breath' became equated with a death wish cast upon the child at birth. The first cry, the first breath, was the kiss of death. This last construction had a significant impact in the analysis. Many aspects of the analysand's identification with her own mother were unfolded and the question of femininity was highlighted. There was a gradual shift for the analysand from the signification of 'bad breath' to simply 'breathing'.

The behaviour of the woman's second child shows how withholding breath can operate at a very early stage in life as a way of showing understanding of a prohibition. It is a way for the child to exercise agency. For example, by with-holding its breath and thereby erasing smell, the child might want to challenge an imposition on its mode of enjoyment. Although the smell of the objects of the oral, tactile and anal drives (milk/breast, urine and faeces, the mother's skin/body) is very present during infancy and early childhood, the emphasis in the prohibitive language of the caregiver will be on the objects themselves and not on their smell. What sort of consequences in the arrangement of the drives could we expect if a child was told 'do not smell your pooh' instead of 'do not touch it'? Or, what consequences would it have on the arrangement of the scopic drive if, instead of admiring a child's appearance in the mirror, the form of their body, etc., the language of the caregiver was to focus on the smell of the child's body? Similarly, when it comes to bath time, much of the available psychoanalytic literature has given significant roles to the gaze and touch of the mother rather than the smell of cleaning and care products, the bathtub (clean or dirty) and, most importantly, the eradication of 'bad' odours through bathing. Some children do not enjoy bath time and the washing of their transitional objects (to use the Winnicottian term), such as favourite blankets or teddy bears, can cause distressing anxiety. In such cases, the smell, the loss of which is feared, is not so much that of the mother or caregiver as that of the child itself. That young children enjoy smelling their own bodies is a common observation. Moreover, making themselves smelly (the reflective voice of the verb 'to smell') is also common practice among young children. In a real case, a child of two and a half years became severely agitated before and during his bath time. The family doctor made various suggestions to the parents to help them handle the child's so-called 'water phobia'. All of them failed to allay the child's distress. More details of the case showed a hidden aspect of the narrative. This young child had no fear of playing outdoors in muddy water or being cheerful in a water park. It was the bath that was to be avoided. The parents were also worried by the child's habit of touching and hiding his own faeces during potty training and of playing with his mother's slipper and putting it in his mouth before falling asleep. We may well think that not bathing and keeping his faeces and mother's slipper for himself was the child's way of keeping his bodily odour and making himself smelly. In other words, this clinical picture may have less to do with a phobia (hydro-phobia) than with coprophilia. More details of the case revealed the mother's own obsession with foul smells, her constant attempts to smell her child, her emphasis on deodorising the child's body and the whole house. It appeared that the child was constantly being sniffed and we may well suppose that this child's behaviour was its way of opposing the mother's intrusion, claiming a different position for itself and trying to do something with the Other's lack of tolerance towards bad odours. In clinical work the analyst might be more inclined to treat the phenomena of the case at the level of drive arrangement in this subject. On a Lacanian understanding, this child was enjoying his experience of olfaction in three voices: to smell (active), to be smelt (passive) and to make himself smelt (reflexive). Other clinicians might label this as a case of coprophilia and take far less interest in investigating the formation of such an arrangement and its meaning for the child. Dolto's approach in such a clinical case would perhaps be to focus on odour and incest. The child, sniffer and sniffed, retained his own smell and Dolto might view smell in this case as helping the child to handle the Oedipal myth, incest and repression. Here, as before, we can also wonder about one's own smell as a way for the subject to separate from the Other and defend against the Other's presence/intrusion. All in all, it seems improbable that the presence of smell and olfaction in a clinical case can simply be reduced to the concept of the drive.

Bad Breath

Breathing is not simply a sign of life – it is life. For a person being alive, both organically and as a speaking being, depends on the autonomous act of breathing air. The air, the object of breath, carries a scent, which sends various messages to the breathing subject. Breathing is always accompanied by olfaction and vice-versa. The circular and rhythmic movement of the air, entering and leaving our body, invites us to reflect on the meaning, significance and impact of our breathing on our formation – on who we are. The language of love and intimacy, metaphor and poetry, have always been rich in olfactory references. It is futile, therefore, to consider breathing or not breathing solely as signs of organic vitality or mortality. As was discussed, in religion and the myth of creation a pure, divine breath sanctions life and this construction has made breathing into a property of language. So, from its Imaginary status (being an organic, vital act), breathing is elevated to the level of symbol and metaphor, organising the Real body. In extreme grief or emotional shock/pressure, pain (Real body) is often expressed by the phrase, 'I can't breathe'. Or, as shown in the mother-and-child clinical anecdote vignette described above, the respiratory system can be invisibly marked by certain signifiers or can escape this symbolisation. The speaking body always speaks of a subjective truth and it never lies. The extreme form of verbal expressions of pain has a respiratory reference because breathing and its absence are the marks of life and death, and breathing can cause a malaise as much as it can manifest a malaise.

This approach provokes reflections on the role of breathing in a social bond with the other. We can turn once again to the clinic of psychoanalysis and resume the exploration on breathing and halitosis at the level of subjective experience and its interpretation. The first of the two cases that I will present below revolves around a phobia concerning the subject's own bad breath. In the second case, the patient, who was coprophilic, suffered frequent anxiety attacks after starting a love relationship with a woman where halitosis was highly eroticised. In the first case, breathing was involved in a phobia around a particular bad odour and the phobia was acting as a rampart against breach of a fundamental secrecy (a forbidden jouissance). In the second case, the subject's mode of jouissance was a 'breath play', sometimes called erotic asphyxiation or asphyxiophilia. The subject was creating a repetitive scenario at many levels of his life, including his sex life. The analysand's own interpretation of his auto-erotic asphyxia was as a recreation of an arrangement through which he experienced a 'euphoric state' of being loved (a fundamental wish of all human kind). It was a solution he had constructed to approach the impossibility of being desired and he connected his practice with a radical rejection that he had experienced from his mother soon after his birth.

By bringing these two cases forward here we will be better able to approach the question 'What is breathing?' from a psychoanalytic perspective.

Case I.

The analysand was a highly educated man in his late thirties. The main complaint that he brought to analysis was erectile dysfunction. He had an obsession with the bodily and breath odours of women, which made it impossible to have sex with a woman unless she wore perfume or used deodorant. He believed that his compulsive masturbation was his solution to overcome his anxiety at not being able to orgasm. His masturbatory practice depended on the smell of his own anal or other bodily wastes. As the work continued, the focus of his narrative shifted to his obsession with his (imagined) halitosis. More detailed materials showed that his fear was, in fact, a fear of contamination/penetration – fear of transmitting dirt or being made dirty by others, as if his body penetrated or was penetrated by bad odour, particularly via breathing. He termed this 'an unwanted invasion to my inside'. As the analytic work developed, his odour phobia crystallised around having or not having control over his sexual urges. He had a foot fetish and the image, which he used during masturbation, of touching women's feet was in strange juxtaposition with his fear of being penetrated by women's odours, his coprophilia (towards his own bodily odours) and the phobia of his own bad breath. The phobia of women's odour (fear of being invaded by it) and bad breath were linked in the subject's narrative, and the question 'What is breathing?' was highlighted and led the work for a while. When he was four years old, the birth of a younger brother had distracted his mother's attention from him. He then developed episodes of fever with a fungal cold sore in his mouth. At the time, he had interpreted his halitosis (due to the fungal infection) as the reason for his mother not wanting to cuddle him. In his teenage years, when his body sought sexual pleasure and during his first sexual encounter, he developed a phobia of his supposed halitosis and a disgust at the smell of the women's body. In the analysis, he interpreted these manifestations as a response to the intense rivalry and rage that he had experienced against his infant brother in early childhood. He believed that his childhood construction, when he ascribed his mother's neglect to his own malodourous mouth infection, had laid the foundation for his phobia of halitosis, particularly in his contacts with women. He also remembered calling his little brother a 'stinky little thing'. The question arose whether his coprophilia, directed at the odours of his own bodily waste, was related to bonding with his brother – whether it was intertwined with his love/hate for his brother. The analysand had treated this brother as his ego ideal throughout his childhood and adolescence and maintained close ties with him in adult life. The analyst singled out 'breathing' as a signifier, decontextualising it in his narrative and posing it back to him as a question. The first immediate chain of associations with 'breathing' concerned questions of agency, control and autonomy, as if breathing had never been an autonomous practice, but was more like an imposition on his being, and particularly when breathing was associated with the olfactory reference. However, there was another layer to the breathing, which involved secrecy in the history of the subject's family. His parents had a legal problem and for the sake of their children's future they had repeatedly warned both of their sons not to 'breathe a word' of this secret to anyone. The analysand found a connection between this matter – a prohibition of forbidden words, which could have grave consequences for this family – and his phobia around his own bad breath. In his case, fear of halitosis was the kiss of death that sealed the lips of oblivion.

Case II.

A middle-aged man had just started an intense love relationship with a woman much younger than him. His panic attacks and depressive mood were triggered soon after the start of their relationship. More details of his symptomology revealed that the first anxiety attack followed an instance of erectile dysfunction during sex. He practiced auto-erotic asphyxia and wanted his girlfriend to practice it with him, which had created serious tension between them. The analysand was the fourth child of a single mother who was an alcoholic and was antipathetic towards her boy children. She had refused to breastfeed him and his infancy was highly traumatic. He was taken away from his mother for some time by his aunt, but was returned to her when he was about five years old. The mother's physical abuse included half-smothering him and keeping him upside down as an act of punishment if he was naughty. He had found it very difficult to breathe on these occasions and once he nearly choked. He was taken away from her again by the social services. Later, he pursued an obsessive interest in submarines and made a successful career for himself in the submarine industry, where his expertise was related to air and lack of air. The practice of playing with his breath had begun in his late teens and this auto-erotic practice was his main way of reaching orgasm. His new girlfriend was appealing to him physically and he described her as 'naïve and caring' towards him. He enjoyed bathing her and referred to this activity as having sex.

In the analysis, he took a special interest in why his mother was so violent towards him and eventually interpreted it as her way of dealing with rage against his father. This new meaning had an impact on his approach to the question of love, opening the way to an interrogation of his sexual problem. He linked his fascination with choking to his mother's punishments. He had the idea that he should have been choked and not born alive and his maso-chistic activities were based on the same premise of not having the right to be alive. Death or the threat of being dead had kept him close company since early childhood and he had found a double meaning of love and hate. The near-to-death experience (through being choked) was equated with love and being worthy of life. So, it was not breathing but the lack of it (a minus) that gave a meaning to life. Playfulness around the practice of asphyxia was his access to life. The kiss of death was his joy of life.

The Nose and Breathing

We have already discussed the nose as a sense organ (the organ of olfaction) in an earlier chapter. Here, we want to go back to the symbolic definition of the nose in literature and philosophy as part of the breathing faculty, in order to say more about breathing. Since Antiquity, the nose has not only been recognised as the organ of breathing but also as the passageway of the soul, as it comes to or departs from the individual at the start and end of life. Moreover, it was an organ closely associated with intellectual capacity (be-ing close to the brain), with intuition, personality and even luck in life. The Greeks and Romans associated the nose with wit and with the sense of disgust and humiliation (Clements, 2015). So, the nose, the vessel of breathing, has traditionally been linked with the intellectual life of the subject. The equiva-lent of the Greek words for 'nose' ('rhis' or 'mukter') and the Latin words ('nasus'/'nares') in the Middle Persian language (Sassanid Pahlavi or Parsig) is 'winig', which has become 'bini' or 'damagh' in new Persian. 'Damagh' has an Arabic root meaning 'brain' and in new Persian, the word renders other meanings, notably intuition and insight, in addition to meaning the nose. As discussed earlier in this book, the latter meanings are linked with the sense of smell and smelling. So, breathing through the nose is associated with a rich panoply of meanings that add to the linguistic values of breathing and empha-sise its direct connection with life, both actual and symbolic. Breathing is life, love/intimacy, sacredness, secrecy, health and sanity, freedom and (we now see) also intelligence and insight.

The idea of the nose as a passageway deserves special investigation. Although breathing is an automatic process, in the sense that a subject does not actively think about it, any disturbance or interruption of the process can cause great distress. The nose as a passage, which purifies, moisturises and warms up the inhalation, plays a significant role in the breathing experience. Illnesses that affect the functionality of the nose can cause distress in the upper respiratory system, sleep deprivation or chronic fatigue as the supply of oxygen to the brain is disturbed. Such conditions not only have an impact on our behaviour, but can also leave a mark on the formation or non-formation of a symptom or the arrangement of the drive.

In the philosophical account of the nose and the soul, the nose is a passage that acts as a bridge between the inner world of the subject and a higher being. The transcendence of a soul happens through the nose. Moreover, the nose was considered as a pathway, which conveys external stimuli into the brain. As was shown, in various languages words that mean 'smell' have a linguistic affinity with intuition and consciousness and in Persian and Arabic, the same word is used to mean 'nose' and 'brain'. The nose can also be thought of as the passageway for release and relief. Almost without our being aware of it, our body experiences a sense of release whenever we exhale air from the inside of our body down the nostrils to the outside. This sense of release may well be behind the sequences of ideas, which connects breathing with a sense of freedom and movement. It is therefore unsurprising that we have many breath-related expressions that express freedom or the lack of it, as when we talk of 'breathing the air of freedom' or of the 'suffocating' atmosphere in a repressive society. It seems that, transculturally, breathing and freedom go hand in hand.

One of my patients who was suffering from panic attacks and chest tightness, had suffered from a recurrent rhinitis in her early childhood. It was evident from her memories of that time that she had also been in the habit of putting things into her nose and hiding them there as a young child and the activity of hiding, in her case, was a way to exercise her freedom. Later, in adult life, she had a history of fleeing from her love relationships with a sense of panic and her panic attacks were associated with a feeling of 'being stuck'. It became clear during the analysis that she had an unconscious intention to put herself in situations in which she was bound to 'get stuck'. She interpreted this pattern as 'I hide to be found!' The patient was highly sensitive to smells and reacted with disgust to any bad odour. Talking about her breathing and particularly her nose, she expressed the thought that the nose had been eroticised in her family's discourse. The nose was referred to as 'the key to beauty in a person's face' and the shape of the nose came first in any description of a beautiful face. This aesthetic significance of the nose was in addition to its role as a hiding place. Reacting to the familial obsession with the shape of the nose, she had cosmetic surgery carried out on her nose soon after she turned eighteen years old. The first operation had gone wrong and she had to repeat the process again a few years later.

The nose in this analysand's narrative had interesting connections to being stuck and to hiding in addition to its role in olfaction. Beads and beans were the main objects she had put in her nose as a child and it emerged in the analysis that a chain of sexualised signifiers had a major influence on her mode of being. Her obsession with beads and precious stones was related to her father's having another family in addition to the family into which she had been born, and her panic attacks had started in her adult life after her father had been diagnosed with a terminal illness. Expressed in Lacanian terms, it appeared that the Name-of-the-Father, which finalised the status of her symptom, was the 'jewellery bits' – the precious shiny objects which she had hidden in her nose and which symbolised the nose as both a container and a safe place. The scopic drive (the appearance of the nose, hiding and exposing), the anal drive (penetrating and retention) as well as the olfactory drive (sensitivity to smells) were highlighted in this case. Her professional life, which involved giving consultations to others, was also related to her obsession. This happened via treatment of the nose as a 'passage', since in her job she helped people find opportunities for movement and new pathways and options in business. One of the last things she said in her analysis was: 'I have a good nose for the business.' The nose as a passage (including, by virtue of its location, a passage to the brain), as eroticised and as a place for hiding things, created a link between hiding and intellectualisation. As noted above, her mode of enjoyment was driven by the fantasy *of being hidden in order to be found* in a place where she was 'stuck'. In the course of the analysis, her anxiety shifted and grief over her father's death subsided. She came to the view that her nose was a passage to her brain, emphasising movement rather than being stuck. Release and freedom, without an urgent need for the Other's gaze (her father's, in her case), emerged as new themes in her narrative.

What is Breathing?

Having exploring different aspects of the act of inhaling and exhaling air, we should now ask: What is breathing in psychoanalysis? Up to this point, we have been focused on olfaction and on breathing only as related to olfaction, but breathing has validity from a psychoanalytical perspective as an act independent of olfaction and it is in this light that it will now be considered.

Already, in this chapter, we have avoided any reduction of breathing to olfactory experience. Indeed, there may be a whole separate book to be written on the subject of breathing as relevant to psychoanalysis. Certain qualities of breathing have already been highlighted for better understanding of how the life of a subject is highly dependent on the air he or she breathes in and out, and we have wondered about the impact on the formation of the subject of the unconscious of the narrative around the act of breathing, as well as breathing itself being a narrative. Dysfunction or illnesses of the respiratory system have a serious impact on the level of the Real body. The fear and anxiety induced by pain related to the respiratory system indicates the Real aspect of breathing, and patients who suffer from pulmonary complications such as asthma, emphysema, COPD or PE (pulmonary embolism), or pneumonia (lung infection) often complain of anxiety about dying. They find it difficult to fall asleep and usually experience some form of insomnia. The fear of 'not breathing' is indeed an ominous thought. Medical experts might blame it on the side-effects of medication or chemical changes in the body that cause uneasiness, irritation or anxious mood in these patients. However, listening to their accounts of distress or pain, the narrative is focused on fear that they will suddenly stop breathing in their sleep.

There are patients without any underlying problem of the respiratory system who suffer sleepless nights due to a fear of not being able to breathe, and worries over apnoea or loss of breath (awake or asleep) is one of the most common and upsetting symptoms of anxiety attacks. The feeling of tightness in the chest is also related to the respiratory system rather than to the heart and blood circulation. So, the chest is symbolised as the locus of breathing. Although, we know from physiology that breathing is centred on the brain stem, the breath of life for our speaking beings comes from the chest. In poetic language, the chest (or breast) is usually referred to as the reservoir of love, pain and secrecy, and breath is also symbolised using those signifiers. The foundation of the symbolic meaning of our being, inside and outside, is marked by the inhaling and exhaling of air. We hold our breath to protest against the Other's imposition, we do breathe exercises to cope with the stresses of modern life, we campaign for pure or less polluted air in the political space, and we call our loved one 'our breath'. All these symbolic constructions of inhalation and exhalation testify not only to the symbolisation of breath, but also to the impact of the organic, vital act of breathing on our introduction to the symbolic order.

In the clinic of psychoanalysis, anxiety is one of the effects associated with breathing. When somebody is anxious, their breathing is faster and shorter than usual, and tightness of the chest – another symptom of anxiety – is associated with breathing. Sadness, despair or grief also find expression in relation to breath (the sigh is a sound created by exhaling). Alteration of breathing in moods of anger and fear is an experience common the most people. There would also be much to say about the emotions that can be evoked by singing or directing the breath through a musical instrument (flute, trumpet, saxophone, etc.). Breathing, either in the form of exhalation to communicate an emotion or in a work of music, can act as an invocation, addressing the other no less successfully than olfaction.

We might then ask: Can breathing influence the arrangement of the drives? It certainly can. Breathing has an impact on a speaking being in the domain of language. As was already discussed in this chapter, breathing, like olfaction, has been symbolised in many different ways. Breathing does not have the structure of a drive on its own, but it can mark the drive montage.

As discussed earlier, in Ernest Jones' account, it was the movement of air as such, without specific attachment to respiration, that required treatment in the light of drive theory.

With or without olfactory experience, breathing is not only vital in our organic life. It also sits in the core of our being and pervades the vocabulary that we use to talk about sexuality and mortality. From our understanding of the basic structure of the symbolic, inside and outside, to the formation of our symptoms and the drive montage, breathing has a life as a part of language as well as in physiology. This can be elaborated through some examples and observations regarding the absence (or fear of the absence) of breathing. They will be the subject of the next section.

Breathing and the Drive: Asphyxiation, Choking and Strangulation

On the 7th February 1994, a British MP was found dead in his home. His body was naked, other than a pair of stockings and a garter. His head was covered by a plastic bag, an electrical cord was tight around his neck and he had an orange in his mouth. It was judged to be a case of accidental death by autoerotic asphyxiation. Such fatal incidents are not unfamiliar in forensic medicine. Such accidental death from asphyxiation can occur through an autoerotic act or be caused by a partner. Does hypoxia (the reduction of oxygen intake below the level required for proper organic function) intensify sexual pleasure due to physiological factors? Or might there be other reasons why this practice offers particularly intense sexual gratification for some people?

Breathing is life and, as will be discussed later in this part, its presence or absence is more than a sign of life and death in the actual, organic, physiological sense. It relates to a subject's sexuality and mortality. As an attempt to play with the vital act of breathing, choking (as an erotic act or an act of violence that attempts to take someone's life) can be read as an act related to grief, guilt, shame, rage, love and hatred, violence and above all, anxiety around the sense of our mortality. It is a practice, which can be playful, dangerous or can operate as an act of self-punishment in order to address guilt. A patient whom I encountered a few years ago, suffered from a tormenting series of day dreams in which he attempted to kill people around him by strangulation. He wanted to be sectioned in order not to act upon such thoughts. The details of his intrusive thoughts revealed that he was particularly hypersensitive towards people's laughter and loud voices, since he assumed that they were ridiculing and humiliating him. This subject had endured an eventful and traumatic childhood, punctuated with violent acts towards him and other members of his family. His father and uncle had been hanged as capital punishment for drug smuggling and, at a young age, he had witnessed his nanny's cardiac arrest and choking (he remembered and recounted to the analyst the bloody foam that came from her mouth). Before this incident, he had once almost drowned and his nanny had rescued him. After the death of his nanny, he developed a secret practice of choking the ducklings and chickens on his family farm. His work as an adult was related to breathing and inhaling. We might ask: What did breathing and choking really mean to him? At what point had his intrusive, obsessional thoughts arisen and what was the function of those thoughts around the interruption of breathing?

Turning to the theme of murderers whose technique is strangulation and whose criminal acts had a sexual motivation, we might ask: What was the stimulation they obtained from the act of killing through obstruction of the victim's airways? Enjoyment of the victims' pain and suffering before death is a common theme in such cases, although there are many variations. The accounts given by Anatoly Slivko, a Soviet serial killer, of the enjoyment he obtained from the final moments of the young boys whom he killed by strangulation are very striking. He ascribed the origin of his murderous career to witnessing the aftermath of a traffic accident, in which a young boy was severely injured. Slivko obtained orgasmic enjoyment from the scene and believed that it had somehow enabled him to forget his own painful childhood for the first time.

It is not uncommon to hear from the couch that, in couple sex, the partner's hand around the subject's neck provokes more intense sexual pleasure. One possible way to interpret this is that the touch of an area so crucial to breathing (the neck) is felt as erotic. Playing with breath is closely associated with control over the other partner, and many testimonies of such sexual practices emphasise this controlling aspect, which goes as far as absolute control over the person's life. Breathing, after all, is a sign of being organically alive as well as having a resonance in language as a metaphor for liveliness and freedom. The fact that we speak of being 'breath taken' when we are stunned or astounded by something outside our usual experience shows how language takes up the theme of interrupted respiration. The French expression 'la petite mort' ('little death') is used to refer to the momentary loss of consciousness that goes with sexual orgasm or with the feeling of release that immediately ensues, and it seems that a similar sensation is experienced in the holding or obstruction of breath in some sexual practices. Holding and then releasing is a modality, which can be exercised to generate enjoyment. It is a modality that can also operate through the circuit of the anal drive: the retention of urine or faeces offers a clear parallel with the holding and releasing of breath.

To choke, to ask to be choked or to choke oneself are three planes of a drive correlated with breathing and these behaviours show how the act of breathing, as an essential marker of being alive, can be understood as a drive in the context of human sexuality. Our conclusions are that breathing has presence in language in the form of a signifier, that there is a sense of control or agency in breathing, that there is a relation between breathing and other forms of drive montage (anal and tactile), and that a repetitive pattern of holding and releasing (or holding the breath followed by a sexual release) is characteristic of the sexual employment of breathing.

Young children, to their parents' consternation, sometimes purposely take objects into their mouth and swallow them. They may also insert things in their nose and thereby obstruct their breathing, as was the case of the female analysand discussed in the last section who, as a young child, had inserted beads in her nose. Such behaviour is, indeed, one of the most frequent causes of paediatric emergencies and a major cause of concern for parents. Experts have linked the urge of young children to take things into the nose or mouth with curiosity about the external world. But what can be the origin of such 'curiosity' and why does it so often involve obstruction of the body's airways. A different approach might be tried: instead of curiosity about the external world based, could the motive force in such behaviour be the child's curiosity about its own body and the corporeal experience it will have as a consequence of its action (obstructing the body's airways). It is notable that small children also insert foreign objects into other bodily orifices and cavities, including the ears and eyes. In all these cases, is the child's curiosity not a part of the circuit of the drive – a curiosity, which has an effect on the body, and therefore incites the subject to seek pleasure from it over and over again?

One possible reading of choking or obstructing the breathing canals would therefore be as a subject's attempt to gain enjoyment from a drive arrangement with a sexual, repetitive nature. Discovering a bodily pleasure through arresting one's breath, strange though it may seem, is similar to the discovery of the pleasure of touching oneself and can be understood under the auspices of the psychoanalytic concept of the drive. It is also important to underline the effect of parental intervention and interpretation on such infantile practice and on symptom formation (if it occurs), since the core of a symptom can be formed on the basis of a subjective interpretation of a particular event much earlier in life. While the drive, which is a subjective arrangement, gives us access to an enjoyment from our symptom, the fantasy, as a bridge between the drive and symptom, is an unconscious scenario or story that a subject repeatedly tells him- or herself in what amounts to a symptomatic act.

Fear or phobia of choking or being choked is one of the most common complaints heard in the consulting room and elsewhere. In the next section, we will see how the phenomenon of choking can be approached outside the concept of the drive.

Phobia of Choking

Just as choking is one of the most common causes of accidental death during sex and of paediatric emergencies, choking phobia is among the most common phobias encountered by clinical services. From the phobia of being choked by food (frequent in anorexia) to a phobic fear of drowning or inhaling polluted air or airborne viruses (ubiquitous during Covid), the range of breathing-related phobias invites us to return to the psychoanalytic literature on phobia.

In the clinic of psychoanalysis, we pay attention in every case to the narrative around a particular problematic in order to approach the fundamental question: What is the subject really addressing? In other words, we try to elicit the scenario of the symptom (fantasy) in order to get to the origin of the symptom formation or to the core of the symptom as the subject's interpretation of an earlier life event. Every narrative point to a particular modality of enjoyment that is interrupted, obstructed or distorted when it is accessed through a symptom. The subject's aspiration to recreate a situation where the enjoyment can be accessed once again can often be observed in the clinic. We will consider a clinical case where choking and breath played a significant role in order to clarify this account of symptom formation and its relation to the concept of the drive from a psychoanalytical point of view. We will see that there is much more to choking as an erotic practice than might be thought when it is dismissed as a mere variety of 'kinky sex'.

An analysand who was an ear, nose and throat specialist by profession came to me for analysis after discovering that his wife had been involved in a long-running affair. His initial symptomology was persistent insomnia, avoidance of eating and a cough. He had developed a phobia of choking after he almost choked on a roast beef sandwich. After a preliminary series of meetings, he was able to approach the reasons for his symptoms. His insomnia and food avoidance had improved since entering the analysis, but his nervous cough had persisted. Exploring this symptom led him to his mother's phobia of her children choking on food or drowning, which prompted her to impose rigid restrictions on her children's eating habits and to forbid them from taking part in any water sports. She suffered from diphtheria in her youth and vividly remembered her pain when she struggled to eat and to catch her breath. The flare-up of phobic symptoms marked a difficult patch in her relationship with the analysand's father, due to his infidelity. The analysand interpreted his choice of profession as his strategy for symbolically curing his mother's suffering. Choking or, to be more precise, exaggerated fear of choking in the previous generation, on his mother's side, had formed the core of his symptom. In his choice of career, he had followed in the footsteps of his father, who was a doctor.

In another case, we find a generalised phobia of choking, either on food or through drowning. The young lady in the case entered analysis to try and deal with persistent anxiety and restlessness. She was in her mid-twenties when she experienced the first of a number of serious massive panic attacks that left her unable to leave home. In the description of her attacks, she referred to the sense of a dark shadow suddenly overwhelming her. This reminded her of a phobia of darkness and of seeing black shadows, which she had experienced when she was about four years old. Her 'black phobia' became the focus of the work and was found to be related to a phobia of choking, which had developed later in life. As a young child, she used to hold her breath when she experienced fear of darkness: the breath holding was her intervention for controlling her fear. The phobia and reactive behaviour seemed to have a real origin in something of which she had no conscious memory: when she was two years old, she had almost drowned in a swimming pool and had been rescued by her mother, who jumped into the pool to save her despite herself not knowing how to swim. The two of them were pulled from the pool by the analysand's uncle. She was told that she had 'blacked out' and then returned to consciousness after a few minutes. She thought that her black phobia might have something to do with this semi-drowning experience.

However, the phobia also had another possible origin. The analysand's mother had lost her own father around the time of her daughter's black phobia and used to sleep in the child's room during the first few months of her grief. Was the 'black' perhaps the colour of the mother's grief or an excessive sense of closeness that the child wanted to distance herself from? Her 'choking phobia' had gradually replaced the 'black phobia' and was connected with occasional periods of anorexia that she had experienced from a young age. The anorexia was not due to a compulsion to keep food out of her mouth or stomach, but was centred around swallowing and was set off by a phobia of choking on solid food and then also on liquids. More details of the context of her choking phobia revealed a strong link with the loss of a significant Other. The intensity of the analysand's panic attacks in adult life could be put down to the lack of a phobic object that would limit the development of anxiety.

There are strong similarities between the case of phobia just described and phobias in two famous cases: psychoanalytic histories, *Little Hans* (as the case is usually known) and *The Piggle*, by Freud and Donald Winnicott, respectively. I looked in detail at Little Hans's phobia in my previous book, *Lacan, Mortality, Life and Language: Clinical and Cultural Explorations* (Jazani, 2021). I will therefore focus here on a reading of *The Piggle*, focusing on the question of phobia and its function as a subject. What can be seen in this case is how, under certain circumstances, a child struggles with an overwhelming presence of maternal (primary) jouissance that is present in the name of care, moral duties and values, familial secrecy or unprocessed grief. The question of a free and safe space becomes urgent and the child is left 'gasping for air', finding it extremely difficult to claim a position apart from the significant Other. Breathing freely, away from this excessive mode of jouissance becomes almost impossible.

The Piggle

The Piggle (her real name was Gabrielle) was brought to Winnicott in January 1964, aged 2 years and 4 months, suffering from a 'black phobia' (Winnicott, 1977). Her parents brought her by train from outside London to see Winnicott. Initially she did not want to be called by her own name, insisting on being called 'baby' or 'mummy'. This was interpreted by her mother and the analyst as jealousy towards a recently born younger sister but we can also wonder about the terms 'baby' and 'mummy' as referring to positions and not simply as an act of naming or avoiding being named. Was the child not trying to find her own space in the face of maternal desire? In the second consultation, as can be read in the case history, she challenges Winnicott's interpretation when he told her, 'You want to be the only baby', replying, 'I'm a baby too!' as if calling on the analyst to recognise her position.

Deborah Anna Luepnitz, a clinical psychologist and author, interviewed Gabrielle in a meeting that took place in London in 2015, when the former analysand was in her fifties (Ref. The name of the Piggle: Reconsidering Winnicott's classic case in light of some conversations with the adult 'Gabrielle')'. It emerges from the interview that Gabrielle's mother had felt jealousy towards her own younger brother, who was favoured as the male child, and we may wonder whether Gabrielle was not following her mother when she felt this urgent need for recognition (Luepnitz, 2017).

Gabrielle's mother had been a German-speaking Czech refugee from Nazism and her father was Irish. Both parents were immigrants to the UK. Gabrielle's mother's name was Bedriska (Czech for Frederika). She was described by her daughter as a brave woman who crossed borders (both international borders and borders in the sense of rules) and had been an outstanding skier. As a young woman who had recently arrived in England, she had volunteered to help the rescue services in London during the Blitz. Gabrielle was her mother's first child and had been given the first name Esther after a great-aunt who had been killed at Auschwitz, but the grief attached to the name made it too hard to bear. Gabrielle's mother had become a child psychotherapist (Kleinian and then Winnicottian).

Gabrielle explained in the interview that her childish word 'babacar', which Winnicott interpreted as a term meaning 'baby' (referring to her little sister), actually referred to Baba Yaga, a witch and phallic-mother figure in Russian and Slavic folklore. Gabrielle's father, a fellow of All Souls College in Oxford, is reported to have been the first-ever fellow of All Souls to get married. He was 12 years younger than her mother and had a stammer. Gabrielle's mother was 'The Woman' for him. Luepnitz notes the father's stammer and mother's thick foreign accent when speaking English (reported by Winnicott in *The Piggle*).

Gabrielle, as the Piggle in Winnicott's case, had apparently told her mother: 'You are black and you make me black!' (ref) One can see this as her endeavour to leave the maternal nest in the early phase of the Freudian Oedipus complex. Winnicott reports her playing with her father in the consulting room and interprets her play as being born from her father's body. She was described as very joyful in that moment, and we can infer that she was starting to use the function of the Name-of-the-Father as a separating agent. However, this is a difficult process. On one occasion almost 6 months after starting her treatment with Winnicott, she tells her father to stop making her black and instead we see Winnicott described in her narrative as someone who has helped her to tie up the black mummy (this was referred to in a letter to Winnicott from the mother). Luepnitz links the black mummy to the mother's grief and unspoken trauma due to the fate of her Jewish family in Nazi-occupied Europe, but is it not also a manifestation of her overwhelming presence for her daughter?

Similar to Freud's approach in the *Little Hans* case, the birth of a sibling is given an important space beside the Oedipal triangle in the reading by Winnicott of the case. However, there seems to be far less stress on the effect of jealousy on the symptom and the formation of desire. His approach tends to neglect the subject's own agency in forming a symptom (a phobia). A pointed out by Luepnitz, it is also notable in both *Little Hans* and *The Piggle* that stories of previous generations seem to have a strong echo in the outcome of the Oedipus Complex and prove even more important than jealousy or rivalry between siblings.

Later in the work, we see how cleverly Piggle (Gabrielle) finds a solution to position herself in her surroundings, using a key as a symbolic object, with which she locks herself and Winnicott in and out. Here we see a strong desire for separation from the Other, and she eventually finds a way to make this separation. She also finds an exit from Winnicott's treatment, particularly when he aligns himself too much with the primary, excessive jouissance. She then becomes shy about the treatment, suggesting the creation of a fantasy to ward off castration anxiety.

Piggle enters the Oedipal Complex like any other child, although her father's presence in the family might seem to have been less strong than the mother's. On one occasion, the young child mixes him with her maternal uncle, Tom, who was ten years younger than her mother and so similar age to her father. As reported to Winnicott, one night before going to sleep, she said: 'I don't know who is uncle Tom and who is daddy.' The father had a stammer, was shy and seems to have looked up to his older wife. But over and above the father's possible weakness in separating the child from the mother (as highlighted in Lacan's take on the *Little Hans* case (ref Lacan, Seminar 4)) there is the unanalysed symptom on the mother's side: something that it is forbidden to speak about, which Luepnitz highlights as the mother's grief after losing family members in the Holocaust. Luepnitz draws our attention to what Piggle says to her mother: 'Mummy, cry about the babacar!' So, it seems that the effect of an unanalysed symptom speaks out in the child and there are perhaps questions to be asked about the mother's desire, into which the child was born. Why was she named Esther but called Gabrielle? Both parents were in analysis and we might even speculate that the child's phobia gave the mother something to be worried about in a way that diverted her from an unsullied and doting relationship to the child, thereby facilitating the child's separation from the mOther when the father in the family was not capable alone of instituting this separation and the insertion of the symbolic law.

Babadook: Do Not Breath a Word

In the last clinical case that I want to discuss in this chapter, the analysand was tormented by a phobia of being strangled. His fear was particularly acute when he found himself in open, empty public spaces and imagined being attacked and strangled by a stranger. More details from the case revealed that he had long-standing grief over the death of his father, who was killed by a respiratory complication after a medical error at a hospital where he was being treated. The analysand, who was six years old at the time, had witnessed the death and particularly remembered his father's helplessness as he gasped for breath. His family had obstructed the process of mourning – nobody 'breathed a word' about what had happened. As in the case of Anatoly Slivko, a childhood experience determined a particular way in which the subject obtained sexual satisfaction in later life. Fortunately, it did not involve the criminal cruelty of Slivko's case, but the analysand engaged in breath play with his sexual partner. So, the traumatic scene in childhood had an impact at the level of the drive arrangement as well as returning to the subject as intrusive thoughts.

The analysand's agoraphobia appeared to be his rampart against a sense of mortality, but the patient had not been able to form a symptom as would have happened if his development had followed a neurotic course. The Name-of-the-Father was not taken as an ally to finalise the status of a symptom.

The case made me think of an Australian horror film by Jennifer Kent, *The Babadook* (2014), which also tells of a phobia that arises from the suppression of mourning and a subject's difficulty in fabricating a meaningful medium (symptom) through which their being can be sustained. A mother has brought up her son alone after losing her husband in a car crash on the day when the child was born. She has hidden all the personal belongings of her late husband and never celebrates her son's birthday, which was also the day of his father's death. She has no new relationship or interest, is entirely focused on her child and does her best to keep things unchanged and to keep away from anything that could make a connection with the past. The child loves magic and wants to become a magician. He has a particular interest in making things disappear and then reappear. He is quite aggressive, carries makeshift weapons to protect his mother and himself, and has a phobia of darkness. After reading a children's book called *The Babadook*, about a creature that stalks anybody who has become aware of its existence, his phobia of darkness becomes worse.

I propose that we see the Babadook, the object of the phobia, in a Lacanian manner as that which compensates for the function of the Name-of-the-Father. In the film, the Babadook eventually preoccupies the mother as well as the son, and triggers the grief that she had not previously faced. This confrontation incites her to search for a solution beyond her child. She had previously avoided recognising, acknowledging or dealing with the grief in a way that could have led her to something desirable for her – something beyond her child.

The son acts out on one occasion: his cousin reminds him that he does not have a father and he reacts with angry violence. Not only has his father's death been left unmourned or even simply denied – his own position as a subject in his mother's desire has been denied since the day of his birth since his birthday is not celebrated. His life is overshadowed by his father's tragic death. Although we see how the child has accepted the situation on one level in his daily life, his acting out – throwing his cousin from a tree house in anger at the words, 'You don't have a father!' – shows that he will not tolerate the Name-of-the-Father being set at nought. His mother's death wish is well depicted and spoken aloud by her when she finally faces the agony of grief, acknowledging a haunting unconscious wish: 'You die!' We are not told the back stories of his parents' desires before his birth. All we know is that he was given a space (during the mother's pregnancy and in her apparently loving relationship with the child's father), but this space was threatened by an implied question: 'Why did have to die and not you?'

Thankfully, the boy holds fast to his aspiration to become a magician with the purpose of making his mother happy. Taking care of and protecting her is echoed in his symptoms. This is his solution for breaking out of the primary jouissance. At the end of the film, they both find a way of living with the grief and the boy's phobia is resolved.

Final Words on Smelling and Breathing

From an outside perspective, paying attention to the sense of smell might not seem to have priority in our contemporary time as it has ceased to be our primary help for survival. The most primitive sense of all is the most neglected sensual experience in the literature of psychoanalysis. In the ancient world, however, particularly in the realm of medicine, the olfactory experience occupied a prime location. Breathing, unlike smelling, is the first and last act of life. With such a stark difference in their position as modern human beings; they are intertwined with one another. Both smelling and breathing influence each other's meaning for a subject. Our being is marked by the smells we breathe in and out. Our quality of life depends on the quality of the air we breathe as much as the scents we smell can change or influence our life experience.

My friends' and colleagues' reactions were quite versatile upon hearing my intention to work on smell and breathing. I heard of humorous, fantastical, romantic associations, and sex jokes. Only one friend pointed to the malodourous but almost everyone thought of my work as research literature on perfume and scents. However, what I intended to research was mainly the formative role of olfaction in our subjectivity. Moreover, the playful nature associated with smelling and breathing puts them in the realm of enjoyment and drive. Moreover, I asked what sort of importance we give to this sense among other senses (sight, hearing, touch, taste) as a speaking being. Would it be essential to distinguish it from other senses in light of the concept of the drive? If the founder of psychoanalysis was a woman, how the question of enjoyment gained from the drive arrangement, particularly the olfactory drive, would have been approached? As a sexed being, our olfactory and breathing experience marks our sexuality while our experience of livelihood and mortality depends on them as a mortal being, doomed and privileged to speak. In this book, we attempted to interrogate the place where our ancestors located the olfaction in their daily life as well as their psychical life. In the history of philosophy, we looked for how the olfaction and the olfactory organs (the nose and the brain) were theorised.

A decisive moment, for my own attitude towards these matters, came in the summer of 2020, when I lost my sense of smell. A prolonged deprivation of the olfactory experience due to the aftermath of a long COVID created a space to embark upon a smelly journey through literature; the smelly words! A strange time, when the meaning of the body, in an analytical sense changed. In a conversation with a French friend, the following phrase came up when we were discussing the smell, breathing and sex, all as bodily experiences. How the body was ever-present in its absence, how it got along with our solitude during the lockdowns and how much we needed to protect it against the noble virus. It was when the questions of space, privacy and moving were posed to the body that I said:

le corps a été tout et tue … et fait taire!

"The body has been everything, killed … and silenced! (My own translation)"

The body was silenced, particularly in an olfactive way. It was heard, seen but due to the lock downs, the most primitive and essential marker of a bodily presence was silenced in a social context. Smell, as the sound of the body marking its presence, dead or alive, healthy or sick, its freshness or poor hygiene was made to be silent.

The olfactory drive or/and breathing as a drive were approached from a psychoanalytical perspective by searching the historical and contemporary clinics of psychoanalysis. We asked what shapes such drives takes and how do they influence our mood We have compiled this book in order to discuss various arguments with regard to formulating our response and position concerning the aforementioned questions. In accordance with the ethos of the analytic discourse, it was attempted to create an open but critical space for raising awareness and questions about olfaction and breathing. The chapters in this manuscript intend to demonstrate an alternative approach to the olfactory experience by recognising the effect and consequences of such experience at the level of the particularity of each individual.

Bibliography

Clements, A. (2015). Divine Scents and Presence. pp. 46–60. In: *Smell and the Ancient Senses*, (eds). London: Routledge

Jazani, B. (2021). *Lacan, Mortality, Life and Language: Clinical and Cultural Explorations*. London: Routledge

Jones, E. (1951). *Essays In Applied Psychoanalysis*, Vol II. London: Hogarth

Luepnitz, D. A. (2017). The name of the Piggle: Reconsidering Winnicott's classic case in light of some conversations with the adult 'Gabrielle'. In: *The International Journal of Psychoanalysis*, 98:2, pp. 343–370.

Winnicott, D. (1977). *The Piggle: An Account of the Psychoanalytic Treatment of a Little Girl*. London: Hogarth Press

Index

102 Index

For Product Safety Concerns and Information please contact our EU representative GPSR@taylorandfrancis.com Taylor & Francis Verlag GmbH, Kaufingerstraße 24, 80331 München, Germany

Printed and bound by CPI Group (UK) Ltd, Croydon, CR0 4YY

08/06/2025

01897002-0004